ISLAND LIFE
101
A NEWCOMER'S
GUIDE TO HAWAI'I

ISLAND LIFE 101

101

A NEWCOMER'S GUIDE TO HAWAI'I

JILL ENGLEDOW

Maui Island Press
Wailuku, Hawai'i

Disclaimer

This book is designed to offer suggestions and resources for newcomers to Hawai'i. It is sold with the understanding that the publisher and author are not engaged in rendering legal or professional advice or services and should be used only as a general guide. It should not be regarded as the ultimate source of information regarding life in Hawai'i. Every effort has been made to ensure that this information is as accurate and timely as possible, but there may be mistakes both in typography and in content. The purpose of this book is to entertain and educate. The author and Maui Island Press shall have neither liability nor responsibility to any person or entity with respect to any loss or damage caused, or alleged to have been caused, directly or indirectly, by the information contained in this book.

Island Life 101
A Newcomer's Guide To Hawai'i
by Jill Engledow

Published by:
Maui Island Press
P. O. Box 176
Wailuku HI 96793-0176 U.S.A.

Cover design by Cynthia Conrad
Index by Madge Walls, All Sky Indexing

books@mauiislandpress.com
www.mauiislandpress.com

Parts of this book were previously published in *Maui 101: Your Guide to Island Life* (Maui Island Press, 2005) and in the Maui and Hawai'i *Drive Guides* (Honolulu Publishing Company, Ltd., 2005).

Printed in the United States of America

ISBN 978-0-9765136-1-2

To the memory of my father, Ed Engledow,
who taught me to be a writer
and brought me to Hawai'i,
to the memory of Patty Stewart,
who helped launch Maui Island Press,
and to my mother, Adele Engledow,
who is always there for me.

*

Acknowledgments

Many thanks to those who have helped launch this book, and the *Island Life 101* seminar from whence it grew. These include the kind and helpful newcomers who sat through my focus groups and practice class. My "angels," Patty Stewart, Adele Engledow, and Joelle and Larry Rudin, gave financial and moral support.

Suggestions and corrections came from Dorothy Pyle, Gail Ainsworth, Janie Taylor, Elaine Wender, Laurel Murphy, Maitreyi Light, Bill Harby, Tom Coffman, and Roy Tanaka. Dorothy Pyle, along with two other Maui Community College teachers, Ki'ope Raymond and Hōkūlani Holt Padilla, have answered many of my questions over the years about Hawai'i history and culture. Please note that these folks are not to be blamed for any inaccuracies, and of course the opinions expressed here are strictly my own!

Robbie Alm shared the story of Live Aloha and many bumper stickers. Audrey Rocha Reed lent her speech about plantation camp life, as well as advice on Portuguese food and punctuation. Mary Cameron Sanford, Al Perry, Dave DeLeon, and East Maui Irrigation Co. provided photos. Beth Butler edited the original *Island Life 101 Handbook* and helped choose the fonts. Janie Taylor, patient and helpful as always, did her usual excellent job of copy editing the final version. Cynthia Conrad designed the beautiful cover.

Mahalo to the University of Hawai'i Press for permission to reprint "Hawai'i Aloha" (*Nā Mele o Hawai'i Nei*, by Samuel H. Elbert and Noelani K. Mahoe, copyright 1970) and to Bob Magoon and Keola Beamer for permission to reprint lines from "Mr. San Cho Lee." Thanks to Honolulu Publishing Company, Ltd. for allowing re-use of content published in their 2005 *Drive Guide*.

Contents

Islands in Transition

Hawai'i is more than just another pretty place. It is, in fact, a community with a long and fascinating history that continues to be felt in many ways.

I'm blessed to live on Maui, in an old Wailuku neighborhood where I walk through history every day.

Once, this land was a giant terraced garden, alive with acres of taro in glittering ponds irrigated by the waters of 'Īao Stream. Not far from the hillside where my house sits, Maui's paramount chief once made his home. The army of Kamehameha the Great surged up this hill in his quest to conquer and unite the Islands. A few decades later, at a school just up the street, missionaries educated young Hawaiians. Sugar growers planted the surrounding acres in cane and created a stone-lined irrigation ditch that still flows through the town.

Years ago, I moved into a plantation-style home next door to a lively old Japanese lady with a bent back and a yard full of anthuriums. On the other side, three generations of a multicultural family share one house. Behind me, a large Hawaiian family has grandchildren in and out of the house all day, and traditional Hawaiian music fills the air. The lady on the corner teaches 'ukulele classes, so Saturday mornings see a steady stream of little kids learning to strum and sing in her covered carport.

It is as if I live in a time capsule, in a neighborhood that could have existed decades ago, somehow preserved on an island now frequented by travelers from around the globe.

I came to Hawai'i in 1959, shortly after statehood, and lived briefly in a Waikīkī area known in those days as The

1

Jungle. Indeed, it did look something like a jungle, with little cottages amid lush foliage on quiet streets. I was enchanted by this lovely place. I had no idea that it was already vastly changed from its natural state as a wetland, where taro had flourished in ancient days and ducks paddled in large nineteenth-century rice paddies.

Today, the quiet streets and old homes have been replaced by traffic and high-rise hotels, and only the recently erected historical markers and statues remind us that Waikīkī was once a gracious and peaceful retreat.

When I moved from O'ahu to Maui, in 1968, there wasn't a single BMW on the island. "Maui cruisers" and old pickup trucks laced with rust traveled narrow rural roads. Some folks still drove salvaged World War II jeeps.

Most stores were the mom-and-pop variety. The sugar plantations' retail system had only recently shut down with the closing of the plantation "camps" as the company offered workers a chance to buy fee-simple lots and homes of their own. There were a few hotels, but the population of Maui was only about 38,000; its young were fleeing an island that offered little hope for work.

O'ahu's population was then about 630,000, Kaua'i's 29,000, and Hawai'i Island's 63,000. The state's population totaled about 770,000.

In 2006, according to the *State of Hawai'i Data Book*, Maui's population had grown to 141,320, O'ahu to 909,863, Kaua'i to 63,004, Hawai'i Island to 171,191. The state was home to nearly 1.3 million people. Each year, some 30,000 people move here from the Mainland.

While Maui's population increase clearly has been the most dramatic, followed by the growth on Kaua'i and on Hawai'i Island, O'ahu went through its own growth spurt. During the '80s, there were so many construction cranes erecting high-rises in Waikīkī that they were nicknamed "the state bird."

The growth in population has brought changes to the Islands that are both exciting and troubling.

The exciting part is that Hawai'i is now a world-class community in many ways, connected by jet and Internet to everywhere else on the planet. It is a place of such natural glamour and beauty that it attracts the world's most gifted people, an oasis of peace, tolerance, and prosperity in a world where those qualities are rare. A half-century ago, many of Hawai'i's young people had little choice but to leave the Islands to find challenging and well-paid work. Today, employers search for workers, and opportunity abounds for entrepreneurs.

The troubling part of this rapid growth is the danger it poses to the community that existed before tourism brought millions of visitors and thousands of new residents. What Hawaiian scholar David Malo predicted in 1837 has indeed come true: The overwhelming tide of foreigners that began as a tiny ripple some 200 years ago now is a great wave.

The indigenous Hawaiian people Malo addressed have suffered much since the beginning of Western contact in 1778, as other races flocked to prosper in these Islands.

To Hawaiians, the land is far more than just dirt. It is the 'āina, "that which feeds us." It is sacred. Water (wai) is wealth (waiwai), to which everyone in ancient Hawai'i had a right. It was the malihini (newcomers) of the nineteenth century who introduced the idea of land as a commodity, an item that could be bought and sold.

Devastated by illness, disoriented by change, and out-numbered by newcomers from many lands, Hawaiians somehow managed to preserve at least some of their culture. Their attitude of kindness and hospitality, the aloha spirit, profoundly influenced even the newcomers who were displacing them.

Now, the multicultural society that grew up in Captain Cook's wake is itself threatened by overwhelming change.

As their numbers increase, today's newcomers some-times maintain almost separate lives, often in enclaves where everyone is from similar backgrounds. No longer do malihini enter a pre-existing social system where their place is determined by their relationship to the sugar and pineapple plantations that once controlled Island life. They are not required, as in days gone by, to learn to live with the mores and customs that evolved through the layering of multiple ethnic cultures over the host Hawaiian culture.

A strong sense of belonging and mutual obligation grew within Hawai'i's "local" lifestyle. This spicy stew, in which each of the cultures is appreciated for its own flavor, flourished on these islands far from any other source of sustenance. People who live on islands must be able to depend on one another. Hawai'i's many cultures developed a high level of what sociologists call "social capital," those bonds and networks that build trust between people and make a community thrive.

The idea for this book grew from discussions I participated in when I worked for Hawai'i Community Foundation, a statewide grant-making and donor services organization. We were concerned about the dilution of social capital that might result from the arrival of thousands of newcomers. If these folks failed to understand that Hawai'i's community life and traditions are as important as its physical attributes, we feared the Islands might lose a way of life many cherish, one that could be an example for the world.

The idea of social capital—the social networks by which we connect with our family, friends, neighbors, and co-workers—was a topic of discussion across the country because of Harvard Professor Robert D. Putnam's book *Bowling Alone* (Simon & Schuster, 2000), which explored in detail the decline of social capital in America. Research by Putnam and others has shown that almost every aspect of life, from crime rates to economic productivity to human happiness, is affected by how we connect with each other. In general, the more social capital a community has, the more it flourishes.

People in Hawai'i who talk about social capital have sometimes likened it to the aloha spirit. Its characteristics can be described by words also used to describe Hawaiian values:

- ❖ mālama: to care for
- ❖ 'ohana: family
- ❖ ho'okipa: hospitality
- ❖ 'olu'olu: graciousness, pleasantness, good manners
- ❖ kōkua: helpfulness
- ❖ lōkāhi: unity, harmony
- ❖ kūpono: honest, fair, upright

The pervasiveness of these qualities in Island society gave old Hawai'i a singular charm. Even in the plantation days when an oligarchy ruled communities divided in many ways by class and race, these and other Hawaiian values provided a foundation for a unique society. People who have lived here for many years look back with nostalgia on the gentle days before statehood and jet airplanes changed the character of this place.

Some newcomers are sensitive to the intangible spirit of Hawai'i and strive to live in harmony with all the best aspects of Island life. But with so many new people arriving day after day, the special qualities of Island life are being diluted and marginalized.

Many newcomers to Hawai'i see only the physical beauty of the land, sea, and sky. Some fail to connect to the history and community life of Hawai'i, and never feel at home. Some simply leave. Others, shielded from the necessity to interact with the local community by the new availability of more Mainland-style enclaves, continue to live as they would have anywhere, and wonder why things here are not done as they were back home.

Back in the 1960s, we used to say "the island decides" whether a person would stay on Maui. Through some combination of circumstances, the island itself seemed to welcome or reject newcomers.

Today, the deciding factor often is not how well one's spirit aligns with a particular Hawaiian Island but how much money one has. The overwhelming power of the dollar now determines not only which newcomers stay here but, increasingly, which local-born or longtime residents survive in a place where housing prices more than doubled between 2000 and 2005.

Other prices also soared, from a gallon of milk to a gallon of gasoline. And wages that might seem generous on the Mainland don't go very far in a place where those with deep pockets are snapping up second or even third homes. One recent study showed that in some parts of the state as many as 20 percent of the homes are owned by Mainlanders. Some of these are second homes, sitting vacant much of the year, while others are used as vacation rentals.

Another study, by the University of Hawai'i in 2007, showed that about one-third of Hawai'i households require assistance from the government, private agencies, or relatives to cover everyday living expenses. The study showed that a single parent on O'ahu with two young children would need an annual income of at least $54,161 to cover a no-frills budget, a bit more in Maui County, and about $3,000 less on Kaua'i. Even on Hawai'i Island, the most affordable, this family would need $46,650 to be considered self-sufficient.

Compare this to the average annual earnings in Hawai'i of $37,050, or to the average annual salary of $22,320 for the most common occupation, retail sales. Obviously, life in the Islands is not a vacation for most of the people who live here.

Island Life 101 was written for those who have moved to Hawai'i and now need to learn how to live in harmony with Island culture, and for visitors who love this place and want to learn more about it. If you are not already living in the Islands, this book was not written to persuade you to move here. The Island tradition of hospitality has meant for generations that newcomers are welcomed warmly. Today's reality dictates that potential new residents hear the blunt but necessary truth: The Islands may be nearing some sort of carrying capacity, some invisible limit on the number of people who can live here without seriously damaging the character—and resources—of this place.

Hawai'i is in many ways the victim of its own success. Tourism pays the bills by drawing millions here, and many of those visitors fall in love with the place and want to stay. Chances are you are one of those people; probably you first came here on vacation.

But the holiday ends when you move here. You still have to make a living, do the laundry, and take out the trash. You enter a housing market so tight that families squeeze several generations into one dwelling, set up a tent in the backyard for extra sleeping space, send kids to live with relatives on the Mainland, or simply pull up stakes and move to Las Vegas. Communities have not kept up with infrastructure requirements as the population has boomed. Water resources are drying up; roads are crowded; tempers are short. And the much-cherished custom of welcoming newcomers is under serious strain as locals struggle to survive.

Those who have moved here may already have learned these truths. Those who have not would do well to consider them before making the move.

My Wailuku neighborhood on Maui is lucky in that it has no fighting roosters crowing us awake in the morning. No one slaughters pigs or goats in their backyards, at least not in the years I have lived here. But such situations, annoying or even horrifying to Mainland transplants, do still exist. Country customs and ethnic practices are still part of life here, even in neighborhoods where an urban culture has grown up around a rural area.

The conflict between the old and new probably will continue. The thousands who flow into Hawai'i every year, intending to make their home here, are transforming the Islands. Kama'āina—children of the land—often watch in dismay as newcomers challenge old ways, all the while increasing the demand for land and housing, for space in the schools and on the roads, for water and electricity. Once again, the children of these Islands must leave; this time because they can no longer afford to live here as housing costs rise ever higher.

7

How will the spirit of Hawai'i survive these years?

Population growth is a reality nearly everywhere on the globe. Since Captain Cook's expeditions put Hawai'i on a map, there has been no going back, and the future can bring only more interaction with the rest of the world.

The key, it seems to me, is to create bridges between the kind old ways native to these Islands and the bright gifts some of its new residents bring to the mix.

My hope is that this book will help smooth the way for malihini who appreciate the kama'āina way of life. Those of us who were not born of this land cannot, by definition, be kama'āina. But if we care for Hawai'i and her people, we may become hānai—the adopted children of a loving mother.

A Newcomer's Guide to Hawaiian History

You have just moved to Hawai'i. You love the weather and the beaches; you're still exploring; you're struggling to make a living and make connections. You have enough to do. Why do you need to know about Hawaiian history?

You need to know because you can't understand modern-day Hawai'i without at least a basic knowledge of the past. Hawai'i is not just a little chunk of Southern California that somehow broke off the continent and drifted out into the middle of the Pacific.

This place has a fascinating history that made it what it is today. If you're here to stay, rather than just for an extended vacation, you need to understand your new home. Even the letters to the editor in the local paper will make more sense if you have some knowledge of Island history.

If you are a history lover, you're in for a treat—these little Islands have seen some amazing events and some incredibly colorful characters. Unfortunately for the original inhabitants of the Islands, these events wreaked havoc on the Hawaiian culture, so this fascinating history is also a tragic one. You need to know about that, too, in order to understand many of the social and political issues facing Hawai'i today.

The following pages present an overview of Hawai'i's past, focusing on key points and incidents. Words you'll want to remember are in **bold.** You'll find here explanations that will help you understand the significance of words still in use and historic events still referred to today. You'll come away from this reading with a sense of the past, as well as some context in which to place the issues of the present and to think about the shape of the future.

Locals Know: If you are fascinated by Hawai'i history, get your hands on a copy of Encounters with Paradise: Views of Hawai'i and Its People, 1778–1941, *by David W. Forbes. Produced in conjunction with an exhibit organized by the Honolulu Academy of Arts in 1992, the book includes many pictures never before published. Along with the pictures are Forbes' detailed descriptions of how they came to be created, plus information about the artists. From landscapes that show Hawai'i in its pre-development days to portraits like that of an aged Kamehameha to the modern imagery of twentieth-century artists,* Encounters With Paradise *provides rare glimpses of Hawai'i and its past.*

Where did the Islands come from?

The Hawaiians have several answers to that question.

One important story tells of the sky-father Wākea and the earth-mother Papa, who gave birth to the Islands. Chiefly incest was traditional in Hawaiian culture, and Wākea and Papa were half-brother and -sister. The pair also produced a lovely daughter, whom Wākea seduced. The first child of this union was born deformed, and when buried, sprouted as the first taro plant, or **kalo,** the staple plant of the Hawaiian diet. Their second child was the first **ali'i nui** (great chief) and the ancestor of all Hawaiian people. Thus, the kalo is the elder brother of the Hawaiian race.

Yet another series of tales describes the adventures of Māui the demigod, an endearing hero and trickster who may have been based on an actual person somewhere back in time. Known throughout Polynesia, Māui is perhaps a deified ancestor, long remembered for his strength and creativity. On a fishing trip with his brothers, Māui is said to have pulled the Islands from the ocean floor with a magical fishhook.

Another Hawaiian creation story, the **Kumulipo**, is a 2,077-line chant that tells of creation from the time of primordial darkness just before the moment of conception of the cosmos. It traces the creation and evolution of the Hawaiian Islands and the Hawaiian people, their history, and their gods.

Scientists tell us the Islands rose from a hot spot beneath the tectonic plate, beginning at least 70 million years ago. The Pacific Plate moves about three inches each year to the northwest. As magma continues to well up and build new land, the Islands themselves move.

Hawai'i is part of the 1,600-mile string of volcanoes known as the Hawaiian Archipelago. Islands near the northwestern end of this string are marked only by coral atolls, formed by coral reefs that long ago grew up around each island. Over hundreds of thousands of years, the reef continued to build, while the island itself subsided under the weight of gravity and the wear and tear of erosion. When an island completely subsides beneath the water, leaving a ring of growing coral with an open lagoon in its center, it is called an atoll. This process may take as long as 30 million years.

At the other end of the chain, the Islands still grow. While the volcanoes that formed Kaua'i and O'ahu are extinct and beautifully eroded by time, Maui's Haleakalā is a live volcano, which last erupted several hundred years ago and could someday erupt again. On Hawai'i Island, Kīlauea has continued to create and destroy land in ongoing eruptions, and two others of the island's five volcanoes— Hualālai and Mauna Loa— are considered still to be alive.

Southeast of Hawai'i Island, beneath the sea, the fire goddess Pele is building a new island. This fiery baby will someday work its way to the surface and begin the cycle that millions of years from now will end in a lagoon.

 Locals Know: While scientists have dubbed the emerging island "Lō'ihi," meaning "long," because it issues from a long fissure in the ocean floor, some Hawaiians think the name should be Kama'ehu. The word, meaning "red child," also is the name of the son of Kanaloa, god of the ocean depths.

Life arrives

Seeds of life arrived here over a period of many thousands of years, perhaps blown in by the jet stream, dropped by birds, or floating in on currents. Isolated by more than 2,000 miles from any other landmass, these accidental immigrants evolved into incredible diversity. Hawai'i is home to more than 10,000 native species, more than 90 percent of which occur naturally nowhere else on Earth.

Human activity, beginning with the arrival of the Polynesians, has resulted in a high rate of extinction. (Just imagine the temptation flightless birds must have presented to the original Polynesian discoverers, and you'll under-stand why those birds no longer exist.) The arrival of Westerners, with their cattle, goats, rats, mosquitoes, and eventually bulldozers, resulted in a rapid increase in extinc-tion. Hawai'i now is home to more than one-third of the birds and plants on the U.S. endangered species list. Nearly 60 percent of Hawai'i's native flora and fauna are imperiled; the Islands lead the nation in the number of plant and animal species proposed for listing as endangered or threatened.

Locals Know: Never mind what you saw in Jurassic Park; though it was filmed on Kaua'i, there were no dinosaurs in Hawai'i!

Polynesian pioneers

Humans arrived here by about AD 300. These first arrivals, probably from the Marquesas Islands, were part of a great migration that we think began about 40,000 years ago in Malaysia. Island-hopping ocean explorers, the people now known as Polynesians settled much of the Pacific while European sailors still skirted their continent's shores.

About AD 1000, a second wave of settlers arrived, probably from Tahiti. They quickly dominated the original population. Voyaging continued among the Polynesian islands until about AD 1200. Then, for some unknown reason, voyaging ceased, and the memory of their ancient exploits survived only in stories about legendary ancestors and faraway islands.

The Polynesians found no metal in Hawai'i and therefore had no choice but to be Stone Age people, but that does not mean that they were primitive. In fact, they developed a sophisticated culture, living in harmony with the land and reaching for the highest levels of artistic achievement.

Modern archaeology tells us that the ancient farmers could have grown enough food to feed as many as a million people. Ethnologist Marion Kelly says pre-contact walled fishpond techniques raised the efficiency of natural food chain protein production by 100 times.

Ka po'e kahiko (the people of old) engineered complex irrigation systems to provide fresh running water to their acres of kalo, which were 10 to 15 times more productive than dryland gardens, Kelly says. They built roads such as the sixteenth-century King's Highway that circles Maui, 138 miles long and 4–6 feet wide.

The Hawaiians made the finest **kapa** in the Pacific, pounding tree bark into soft, pliable fabric. Their feather-work was unmatched. Plucking feathers from birds (which were then released to grow more feathers), craftsmen created cloaks, capes, helmets, and lei of great beauty.

The Hawaiians had no written language, but they developed highly evolved oral traditions. Their chants were poetry of depth and subtlety, each remembered and repeated with great accuracy by people who believed that words literally had the power to cause action.

A chant could be a prayer, honor an individual, welcome a newborn, or lament a loss. One of the chant's most important functions was to record the genealogy of chiefs, because one's place in society, and among the hierarchy of chiefs, depended largely upon one's genealogy.

The kapu rules

Four classes made up Hawaiian society: the chiefs (**ali'i**), priests (**kahuna**), commoners (**maka'āinana**), and a slave caste (**kauwā**).

The job of the ali'i was to administer and manage society and to propitiate the spirits and forces of nature that controlled the world. In this animistic culture, the gods permeated nature, taking many forms. There were four major gods, plus thousands of demigods and family gods called **'aumakua**. Today, many Hawaiian families still claim an 'aumakua, perhaps an owl, a lizard, or a shark. The ali'i, said to be descended from the gods, performed rituals that kept nature, gods, and humanity **pono,** or in righteous balance. An elaborate and rigid code of conduct called the **kapu** system protected the sacred nature of the ali'i class and kept order in society.

Ka'iana, an ali'i of Kamehameha I's time

The task of the kahuna was to monitor the work of the ali'i and to ensure that everyone obeyed the kapu, which governed all aspects of life. This class also included the experts who had mastered such arts as canoe making or using plants for medicine.

14

As with many Hawaiian words, the English definition of *maka'āinana* leaves much to be desired, because the Hawaiian word carries connotations of an honorable and important position not expressed by the word *commoner*. One interpretation that does the word a bit more justice is "the eyes that watch over the land."

The kauwā were outcasts, branded from birth by a tattoo on the forehead, and were often used for human sacrifice. Some modern historians question whether this caste actually existed or if it is simply legend.

Described by the artist as "a warrior," this drawing
may actually depict a kahuna.

Mana made the ali'i sacred. Everything in the world had mana, the spiritual power or universal force present since the creation of the universe. In Hawaiian taxonomy and evolutionary theory, all species had some level of consciousness; even rocks had their share of mana. But it was the ali'i who stood at the peak of the system, with the greatest amount of mana.

The kapu system guarded the highest ali'i with rules such as the burning kapu, which functioned as if the kapu chief emitted fiery rays of mana. If someone's shadow fell onto this chief, the offender would have to die; these ali'i sometimes chose to spend their daytimes indoors to avoid this possibility.

Mana could be increased by the intermarriage of high-ranking brothers and sisters. This ritualized incest was a sacred aspect of ali'i life, a merging that magnified mana to bring about new generations of ever-higher rank.

While the ali'i were at the peak of the social system, allegiance went both ways. A sense of responsibility and mutual obligation was woven into the social structure.

Maka'āinana whose ali'i did not fulfill their responsibilities to care for their people were free to leave and find another leader, or even to band together against an oppressive chief. One proverb reminded ali'i, "You are a chief because of your people." When things were going really badly, as in times of military defeat or famine, the high chief whose responsibility it was to keep things in balance might be killed and replaced by another.

Mutual obligation also existed between neighbors and extended family. When Westerners came to Hawai'i, they got the impression that the Hawaiians were a very giving people, and indeed they were, but their system depended upon reciprocity and giving back.

Land divisions fostered this way of being. Though there were several kinds of land division, two whose names are still in common use are **kuleana** and **ahupua'a.**

The kuleana is a smallholding, a maka'āinana home and the surrounding area. Today, you'll still hear people say that something is (or is not) their kuleana, meaning their area of responsibility. The ahupua'a was the basic unit of taxation, under the management of one chief. Many ahupua'a were pie-shaped sections of land, often running from mountain to sea. Everyone within the ahupua'a boundaries had access to resources up and down its length. Its people shared their goods and worked together on big projects. They lived in an intimate relationship with nature and the land, finding everything they needed within the ahupua'a.

On the other hand . . .

In many ways, this well-fed society—with the leisure to decorate their bodies with tattoos, flowers, and feathers, develop poetic chants, and even invent the sport of surfing —looks like a paradise. And if you compare it to life in other parts of the world at the time, it was indeed a good life.

But paradise it was not. The old Hawaiians' view of the universe was very different from ours, and it is unlikely that we'd be comfortable living in their world.

Just over two centuries ago, human sacrifice was still being performed in these Islands. Chiefs fought bloody wars, often ravaging the populace.

Women in particular suffered from the restrictions of the kapu system. Except in special circumstances, women were forbidden to eat many kinds of food, including some of the most succulent in the Hawaiians' limited diet—pork, shark's meat, some kinds of fish. In a place with few sweet foods, women could eat no coconut, and only certain kinds of bananas. They were banned from some beaches, and required to retire to the women's hut during their menstrual period.

Ali'i wahine (female chief) in the fashion of the day

Men did all the cooking—but men and women were then forbidden to eat together, on pain of death. These and other kapu were suspended at certain times, such as the mourning period after a chief's passing. But most of the time, sharing food with the opposite sex could be fatal.

Many modern Hawaiians look back with nostalgia on pre-contact times, and one Hawaiian woman intellectual claims that she would be willing to give up the kapu foods and eating with men in exchange for not having to cook! Yet another points out the disparity between the lives led by Hawaiians of the 1700s, where there was plenty to eat and the nearest bath was just a splash away, and those led by impoverished Londoners, who might starve without anyone paying much attention, and who might go a lifetime without bathing.

The outside world arrives

Whatever the pros and cons of Hawaiian life before 1778, it would all change forever with the visit of the British explorer **Captain James Cook**.

Captain James Cook

In the late 1700s, one chief was close to achieving control of all the Islands. Kahekili, paramount chief of Maui, also had conquered Molokaʻi, Lānaʻi, and Oʻahu, and his brother controlled Kaua'i. Only Hawai'i Island, with more land than all the other Islands combined, remained independent. It was ruled by Kalaniopu'u, a chief who fought many battles with Kahekili and at times controlled the Hāna district of Maui. In January 1778, Captain Cook sighted the islands of O'ahu and Kaua'i, and landed on Kaua'i. Though a Spanish voyager may have happened upon Hawai'i in 1555, the Spaniards recorded an incorrect longitude, so it was Cook's arrival that put the Islands on the map. He named them the Sandwich Islands, in honor of his British patron (the same fellow who gave his name to the sandwiches we eat today).

Things would never be the same again for the people of these tiny, remote Islands.

Captain Cook was a man of the Enlightenment, a key player in the European peoples' efforts to understand their world, and he was on his third voyage through the Pacific. The goal of this particular journey was to find a Northwest Passage above the American continent, which Europeans hoped would provide an easier route between the Atlantic and Pacific. (Though there are passages between the islands of the Canadian Arctic Archipelago, it would not be possible for ships to penetrate them until the twentieth century.)

Happening upon Hawai'i, Cook immediately recognized that the people of these Islands had much in common with those of other Polynesian islands he had visited. He estimated a total population of about 400,000, but modern archaeology suggests the total may have been much greater.

Cook attempted to keep his men from the intimacy that would spread the venereal disease prevalent among them, but that effort failed when a trading party was stranded for the night on the little island of Ni'ihau. When Cook's two ships returned to Hawai'i the following November, he could already discern signs of venereal infection on the people who visited his ships off the shores of Maui. Some think this infection might have come from possible earlier visits by the Spanish. In any case, VD was among the West's first gifts to this isolated island people.

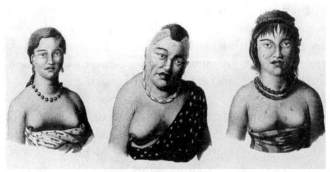

Hawaiian wāhine

Unable to land at the shallow bay of Kahului, Maui, Cook sailed on to Hawai'i Island. There, he was at first greeted as the long-lost god Lono. He stayed for a while to replenish supplies, then sailed away. A storm damaged one of his ships and drove him back to the village of Kealakekua. But the British visitors had worn out their welcome. When a native stole one of his small boats, Cook attempted to force its return by taking the chief Kalaniopu'u hostage. The resulting altercation ended in Cook's death.

 Locals Know: A common story claims that the word **haole,** *usually applied to Caucasians, refers to early newcomers who refused to engage in the Polynesian tradition of greeting by touching noses. Supposedly, Hawaiians decided the newcomers were without spirit, or breath: ha (breath) 'ole (no). In fact,* haole *is an ancient pre-contact word for* foreigner. *It can be applied to other races (haole kepanī, or Japanese) and even to objects or plants (koa haole, an imported weed whose leaves somewhat resemble the native koa).*

Napoleon of the Pacific

Among the chiefs who met Captain Cook was an ambitious young man named **Kamehameha**. When Kalaniopu'u died, he named his son Kiwalao successor, while leaving his nephew Kamehameha charged with custody of the war god Kūkā'ilimoku. This did not satisfy Kamehameha, who set out to become paramount chief, not just of his home island but of the entire chain.

Kamehameha I

In 1790, Kamehameha invaded Maui, at a time when Kahekili was on Oʻahu and his son was in charge of the island. In the famous battle of Kepaniwai, the invaders defeated Maui's warriors through the use of Western cannon Kamehameha had acquired, along with two Western sailors who knew how to use them.

One prize of this battle was the divine chiefess **Keōpūolani**, Kahekili's great-niece. This young girl was at the pinnacle of the kapu system, and Kamehameha's union with her would produce children of the high rank desirable to a chief with dynastic ambitions.

Keōpūolani is known as Kamehameha's Sacred Wife, because her rank was so high as to be considered divine. It is said her husband had to approach her on hands and knees. The two produced three children.

Their two sons, Liholiho and Kauikeauoli, became Kamehameha II and III. A daughter, Nāhiʻenaʻena, was caught in the cultural upheaval as the Western world brought radical changes to Hawai'i. Reared to be her brother Kauikeauoli's wife, she was torn between the old ways and those of the newly introduced Christianity, which forbade such pairings. Nāhi'ena'ena died young, after giving birth to a short-lived child who may have been her brother's.

Kamehameha had twenty-one wives, of whom the most famous is his Favorite Wife, **Ka'ahumanu.** Like Keōpūolani, she was born on Maui, the child of a Romeo-and-Juliet union. Her father was from Hawai'i Island, and her mother from the Maui royal family. After a battle with Kahekili, Ka'ahumanu's parents fled to Hāna, on East Maui, where their baby was born in a cave.

Ka'ahumanu's father, a friend and ally of Kamehameha, gave his daughter to the rising chief when she was ten years old and he was thirty. The girl grew to be tall, beautiful, and brilliant, an appropriate match for the great Kamehameha. Politically well connected on both islands, she held unusual influence for a woman in Hawaiian society, yet still had to obey the restrictive rules of the kapu.

Kamehameha's victory at Kepaniwai was just one step in his struggle to gain control of the Islands. Kahekili still was the most powerful chief in the Islands. But Kahekili was growing old. After his death, Kamehameha, who had in the meantime gained control of Hawai'i Island by killing his cousin, completed his conquest of Maui and invaded O'ahu.

Kamehameha defeated Kahekili's son Kalanikupule at the battle of Nu'uanu in 1795, where the Hawai'i Island warriors forced some of the O'ahu army over the Nu'uanu Pali as others fled into the mountain forest.

Two attempts to invade Kaua'i were unsuccessful, one stymied by stormy seas and the other by an illness that struck down much of his army and which the conqueror himself barely survived. When Kamehameha made it clear that he intended to keep trying, Kaua'i's paramount chief, Kaumuali'i, chose to surrender by treaty rather than risk his island's well-being.

The new kingdom

Hawai'i's first official capital was Lahaina, a seaside village then green and well watered by streams flowing from the West Maui Mountains. But Kamehameha soon found it necessary to spend much time in Honolulu.

Once a dusty little fishing village called Kou, the newly named "Honolulu" (protected bay) was beginning to develop into a commercial center. Its deep, sheltered harbor first was sighted by a Western ship about 1793. It became a favorite stopping point for sea captains and fur traders traveling between Northwest America and China.

Foreign ships filled Honolulu harbor

Never one to miss out on a good business opportunity, the king took control of another O'ahu harbor, this one filled with oysters, which produced pearls of great interest to the newcomers. Kamehameha also took control of the aromatic **sandalwood** trees, growing high in the mountains.

The oysters of Pearl Harbor would soon die, as grazing by newly imported livestock ravaged the land surrounding the harbor and filled its tributary streams with silt. But the sandalwood business began to flourish in about 1810, when sea captains realized its value as a trade item in China.

Kamehameha kept a tight rein on this commodity. But after his death in 1819, the chiefs demanded control of the precious wood in exchange for supporting his young son as Kamehameha's successor.

The chiefs had quickly acquired a taste for consumer goods. The trading system for obtaining these goods from Western ships involved digging a pit the shape and size of a ship's hull. The hole was then filled with a ship's load of sandalwood carried on the backs of maka'āinana from the mountains. The chiefs traded the wood for everything from fine silks to furniture to guns and ships. The maka'āinana, meanwhile, were kept so busy with the chiefs' work that they were forced to neglect their own farming, and their families began to go hungry.

Eventually, the chiefs owed so much sandalwood to the traders that the United States sent a gunboat to demand that the kingdom pay the debt to American sea captains. To do so, the kingdom imposed a tax on every citizen, and its payment resulted in the stripping of nearly every last scrap of sandalwood that once had clothed the mountains.

Hawai'i's first trading commodity had been destroyed, and a culture that formerly lived in harmony with nature had devastated its own land in the quest for imported goods. It was a sad harbinger of things to come.

End of the kapu

The conqueror's death brought about other changes. His widow Ka'ahumanu immediately stepped forward to claim a new place in Hawai'i's power structure as premier, to rule alongside Liholiho. The old king had been a conservative, preserving the ancient ways while adopting the useful new technologies of the West. Ka'ahumanu had other plans.

It had not escaped the queen's notice that, in nearly forty years since the first white men had landed in Hawai'i, they had freely broken the rules of the kapu system with no ill effect. In fact, many Hawaiians had tested the system themselves, notably women who visited the foreign ships and there ate with men, normally a capital offense

Ka'ahumanu had an unlikely ally in her quest to do away with this system that had ordered her people's lives for centuries, while keeping an able and intelligent woman like Ka'ahumanu from fully participating in political life. Keōpūolani, herself at the pinnacle of the system, joined her sister wife in demanding that the young king sit down with them for a feast.

Ka'ahumanu and retainer

Liholiho at first resisted but soon gave in to the matriarchs. Once he had shared a meal with them, the kapu was no more. Conservative elements who fought to retain the old system were defeated in battle. The stones of the **heiau** (places of worship) were tumbled, and the wooden gods were burned. The Hawaiians, already devastated by imported disease, now had lost their spiritual and social moorings.

The missionaries arrive

In a strange conjunction of circumstances, the first Christian missionaries arrived in the Islands within months of the death of Kamehameha I. They landed in Kona, on Hawai'i Island, in March 1820, thinking that the old king was still alive, and having no idea that the native religion had just been destroyed by its own followers. Missionaries continued to arrive for several decades. They were part of the Great Awakening that took place in the United States in the early 1800s. Their mission, in addition to Christianizing these Polynesian "heathens," included the admonition to create "fruitful fields and pleasant dwellings."

Anyone who reads descriptions by the earliest Western visitors will find it ironic, if not laughable, to think that anyone could teach the Hawaiians anything about creating fruitful fields; they were world-class farmers. And some Hawaiian chiefs, when given a choice, preferred to stay in their customary grass houses, using their new Western-style houses to store their Western-style belongings.

But there can be no doubt that, in the decades since first contact, life for the Hawaiians had deteriorated greatly. They were adrift in a world they had never imagined, their shores undefended against imported diseases and foreign adventurers, their social system so weakened by outside influences that its own leaders had discarded it.

It was the urging of young Hawaiian men, in fact, that had inspired this mission by American Calvinists. Several of these young men, sailing off to see the world, found themselves in New England. One man in particular, Henry ʻŌpūkahaʻia, pleaded for a Christian mission to his people.

Missionary Hiram Bingham and convert Henry ʻŌpūkahaʻia

In the beginning: The Word

Soon the missionaries were hard at work with their first great task: creating a written Hawaiian language. These Protestants believed that the way to God was through the Bible. The Hawaiians would not be able to follow that path until they had a written language and a Bible to read.

The chiefs, especially Ka'ahumanu, were quick to see the value of this intriguing new skill. They encouraged the missionaries, who devised an alphabet of thirteen letters, with help from an English missionary who had spent time in Tahiti.

The missionaries were educated, but they were not trained linguists, and they had to make difficult choices. Was that a V or a W? Did that word start with a K or a T? Perhaps it sounded one way on Kaua'i and another in Kona, or perhaps it actually was somewhere in between the sounds that made sense to New England ears.

And that little break in the sound between vowels? Never mind that. Just get those words down on paper; just put that printing press to work.

Indeed they did. The first printing took place in Honolulu in January 1822 in the mission station that still exists as the Mission Houses Museum. Schools sprang up everywhere. The chiefs made laws to encourage literacy, like the one that forbade anyone under the age of twenty-six to marry until he or she had learned to read. Later in the nineteenth century, more than 80 percent of the population was literate, an impressive figure in any time and place.

The first high school west of the Rockies was established on Maui in 1831 at Lahainaluna, its purpose to train young Hawaiian men to become preachers. These young men would need proper wives, so a seminary for girls opened a few years later in Wailuku, safely situated on the far side of the West Maui Mountains.

Spreading the Word at Kailua

In defense of the missionaries

Many people today blame the missionaries for the near-destruction of Hawaiian culture, conveniently overlooking the fact that the destruction was well under way before they ever arrived.

In the long run, Christianity did contribute to this devastation, beginning with the suppression of hula, which the missionaries considered lascivious. They insisted on clothing bodies previously cooled by the touch of trade winds, and persuaded the chiefs to require marriage, one man with one woman, as a prerequisite for sex. And by the end of the 1800s, the Hawaiian language was on the way out as the descendants of missionaries promoted the Americanization of the Islands.

But at the time of their arrival, these missionaries in their New England clothes with their Puritan values and Calvinist suspicion of the Hawaiians' joy and playfulness were among the very few people who came to Hawai'i with good intentions.

Other newcomers came to exploit: to take sandalwood, to provision their ships, to dally with the women and play on the balmy shores as respite from grueling sea journeys. Only the missionaries came to do good. While some point out that they also "did well," it was mostly their descendants who benefited from the combination of

Western parentage and familiarity with the Islands. And, while some of the missionaries were forced to go into business when the sponsoring mission society withdrew financial support in 1863, their original and primary goal was to help a people faced with overwhelming change in an often menacing new world.

One can argue about any evangelical mission as to whether converting people is a beneficial activity; the answer largely depends on one's own belief system. As Christian missionaries, these newcomers demonstrated their faith through their actions at a time when the Hawaiian community had been severely compromised by four decades of contact with less benevolent representatives of Western society.

If the missionaries had not arrived when they did, bringing literacy to preserve in writing the language and remnants of Hawaiian history and even the little aid that nineteenth-century medicine could offer those suffering from imported illness, there might be no trace left today of Hawaiians or their culture.

A fragile kingdom

Hawai'i's rulers certainly needed help to deal with the outside world making its presence felt in the Islands.

The brief reign of Liholiho, Kamehameha II, ended in 1824 when he visited England, contracted measles, and died. Liholiho's brother, eleven-year-old Kauikeauoli, succeeded him as Kamehameha III, with Ka'ahumanu as regent.

The newly arrived missionaries struggled to bring some New England–style order and decorum to a society where the Hawaiians, their young monarch, and his advisors were only too easily manipulated by outsiders interested mostly in lifting a pint and making a buck.

Though things settled down a bit later in the thirty-year reign of Kamehameha III, the kingdom still faced major challenges. These led, in the late 1840s, to a land division known as the **Māhele,** which revolutionized life in the

Islands. Always, the people of Hawai'i had belonged to the 'āina as much as it had belonged to them. No one "owned" the land, except perhaps the king himself, with various levels of chiefs as managers.

This resulted in conflicts between the government and foreigners who wanted to do business the way it was done back home, and who did not hesitate to call on their own governments to resolve their grievances. Hawai'i, it seemed, would have to find a way to cope with the demands of a growing number of foreign businessmen who wanted the security of knowing they could control the land under their operations.

Outside the kingdom, the great European political powers prowled the Pacific, seeking territory to devour. From their point of view, any piece of land not "owned" by someone else was available for them to claim.

Kamehameha III

Tiny and vulnerable, Hawai'i several times lay under the guns of foreign warships, and in 1843 actually spent five months controlled by a British lord who had been sent to sort out a property dispute involving a British national.

Instead, he forced the king to cede sovereignty to Great Britain. Only when the British government sent an emissary to straighten things out was the usurper made to back down, and Hawai'i's sovereignty returned to its king.

The Māhele

By the late 1840s, the king's haole advisors had persuaded him that the best solution to these problems was to institute a system of private property ownership.

The resulting division—the Māhele—gave the king not quite a million acres, the chiefs and the government each about 1.5 million acres, and the common people a disappointing 30,000 acres.

The intention had been for maka'āinana to acquire their kuleana, but in the complicated and confusing division of lands, few people managed to stake their claim, and many who did later traded it for cash. As a result, these people who already had suffered many losses now became landless peasants in their own kingdom.

Today, the crown and government lands comprise what is known as the **"ceded lands,"** some 45 percent of the Islands, now mostly controlled by the state. Some of the ali'i sold their lands (which form the basis for many of the great land-owning corporations today). Others left vast holdings to establish and support such charitable organizations as the Kamehameha Schools and Queen Lili'uokalani Children's Center.

 Locals Know: The process of division that privatized Hawai'i land historically was known as the Great Māhele, but now is often called simply "The Māhele." While the division was "great" in size and impact, many modern Islanders think that "great" may be too positive a word to appropriately describe the loss of land suffered by the majority of Hawai'i's native people.

The last monarchs

Hawai'i's monarchs, like their people, suffered from short lives and impaired fertility because of imported diseases.

Kauikeauoli died in 1854 with no issue and was followed by his nephew Alexander Liholiho (Kamehameha IV), whose only child died at age four. His bachelor brother Lot Kamehameha (Kamehameha V) succeeded him and died without naming an heir. A Kamehameha cousin, William Charles Lunalilo (King Lunalilo), was elected king and died a year later, also without naming a successor.

King David Kalākaua was elected in 1874. The colorful reign of the **Merrie Monarch** was marked by controversy.

Kalākaua

Kalākaua was a bon vivant who loved wine, travel, gambling, and the high life. The king brought hula out of the closet in celebrations that scandalized the missionary set. Presiding over a revival of the Hawaiian culture, Kalākaua was a musician who encouraged traditional practices and documented Hawaiian myth. (The great annual hula festival in Hilo is named the Merrie Monarch in his honor.)

The first monarch to travel around the world, Kalākaua was also the first reigning monarch to visit the United States. He built 'Iolani Palace, at a cost of $300,000. He helped bring about the Reciprocity Treaty, securing favorable trade terms that allowed the sugar industry to flourish and brought some economic stability to the Islands.

Kalākaua's reign was marred, however, by political turmoil and scandal, including one unsavory episode in which the king himself was accused of having accepted an opium license fee from a Chinese merchant. The merchant received no receipts, and in the end did not get the license he sought.

Other problems included the king's love for gambling and his lavish spending, which resulted in his borrowing large amounts of money from California sugar baron and gambling buddy Claus Spreckels. Kalākaua was prone to make frequent and temperamental changes in his cabinet, and sent a ship manned by reform-school boys to Sāmoa in a failed attempt to establish a Pacific Empire with Hawai'i as its leader.

All this was terribly worrying to the growing business establishment, and for the first time in Hawai'i there arose political parties: those (mostly native) who supported "Hawai'i for the Hawaiians" and were anti-immigration, and those (mostly haole) who were in favor of business, sugar plantation expansion, and the importation of laborers to work those plantations.

By this time, the Hawaiian population had shrunk to fewer than 45,000, a drastic decline in the century since Westerners had brought the first seeds of destruction. If sugar planters were to succeed, they needed more workers, they wanted a business-friendly government, and they were quite indifferent to the rights of the natives of the land.

The pro-business "Hawaiian League" party forced the king to sign a new constitution drastically limiting his powers, stripping the voting rights from ordinary poor Hawaiians while allowing some foreigners to vote. It was a strikingly un-American sort of constitution, considering that it was shaped by people who identified themselves with the United States. The Hawaiian League called this a "reform" constitution. King Kalākaua and his supporters named it the "Bayonet Constitution."

In 1891, the king died, to be succeeded by his sister **Lili'uokalani.** Like her brother, Queen Lili'uokalani was well traveled, sophisticated, and intelligent, a musician whose songs are among the most beloved of all Hawaiian melodies.

Lili'uokalani

Along with her brother's throne, the new queen inherited his problems: a dysfunctional legislature and cabinet and an economic depression. Urged on by petitions from her people, the queen attempted to promulgate a new constitution that would return power to the throne, remove the property requirements for voters, and restrict the franchise to subjects of the kingdom.

The overthrow

This was the excuse the Hawaiian League had been waiting for. There had been talk of annexation for many years, but the United States had always refused to take over the Islands. The current U.S. minister to Hawai'i, however, had assured the haole party that, if they could obtain de facto control of the government, he would recognize them. They did, and he did.

It was an almost bloodless overthrow, a coup d'état in which the rebels simply walked in and took over government headquarters while its guards were distracted by the one casualty of the revolution, a policeman who had been shot when he tried to stop a rebel with a wagonload of guns. A U.S. Naval captain, anticipating trouble, already had sent troops ashore, so the U.S. military was patrolling the streets of Honolulu.

Hoping to avoid bloodshed, the queen ceded her authority, under protest, to the U.S. government. She was confident the United States would not allow this injustice to stand. President Grover Cleveland nixed the rebels' plans for a quick annexation, and sent an investigator to Hawai'i.

Based on that investigator's report, Cleveland told Congress he would never submit an annexation treaty to them. With the participation of the diplomatic representative of the United States, he said, "The government of a feeble but friendly and confiding people has been overthrown. A substantial wrong has thus been done which a due regard for our national character as well as the rights of the injured people requires we should endeavor to repair."

Reparation never occurred. Concerned about what might happen to the rebels of American descent if the queen should retake her throne, and facing the possibility of military action in order to force a change, Cleveland left office without restoring Hawai'i's sovereignty. He was replaced by William McKinley, whose Republican Party had less sympathy for the plight of native peoples, and the Hawaiians' complaints went no further.

Denied annexation, the rebels simply formed their own republic. There was a brief counter-revolution, in which the queen may or may not have been involved, and she was arrested and kept captive in her own palace. In 1895, Lili'uokalani abdicated.

The Spanish-American War in 1898 overcame whatever scruples the United States might have had about accepting the gift of these Islands, which included that convenient mid-Pacific coaling station known as Pearl Harbor. Hawai'i was to become an important military outpost of the United States, with the first Army post, Fort McKinley, established just days after the American flag was raised over the palace.

Hawaiian Republic President Sanford B. Dole changed titles to become the first governor of the Territory of Hawai'i.

No one in power asked the Hawaiians what they wanted, and it was a century before anyone took official notice of the petition signed by some 38,000 Native Hawaiians (virtually the entire Hawaiian population) opposing the annexation of their country by the United States. By that time, Hawai'i had long since become a state. How to unravel that relationship and restore sovereignty is a topic under intensifying debate today.

Commerce: The key

At last, the property-owning, sugar-growing, profit-making class had free rein.

The crop that was to shape Hawai'i for the next century was the end product of much experimentation. Many crops would grow in Hawai'i, but it had been tough to find one that would still be worthy of purchase after a long ocean journey and days spent sitting on docks.

Commerce, of course, is always key to the development of a society. In the days of the Hawaiians, before Western contact, a complex network of relationships ensured that everyone had access to all the necessities of life. There was no profit or economic exploitation, simply sharing between the various 'ohana (families) who populated any given ahupua'a.

The arrival of Westerners created a demand for products to supply visiting ships and the availability of foreign trade goods to whet the consumer appetites of people who previously had grown, caught, or made everything they needed.

Hawai'i's first trade goods included fruit and vegetables sold to voyagers famished for fresh food. In 1793, Captain George Vancouver brought the first cattle to the Islands. Herds left to run wild multiplied to form the basis for a ranching industry that supplied visiting ships with meat and hides.

Hawai'i's first major commercial product, sandalwood, was a short-lived success as greed and unwise harvest resulted in its destruction.

A new business, supplying whaling ships, was born in 1820, in many ways a turning-point year for Hawai'i. The old king had died and been replaced by his son. The kapu had been overthrown. The missionaries arrived from New England. And their New England neighbors, the whalers, discovered the Islands.

Searching for whales in the North Pacific, these seamen found Hawai'i a perfect place to take a break each spring and fall. Grog, women, and fresh food (especially the delicious white potatoes grown in the Kula district of Maui) attracted hundreds of the ships. It is said that, at times, one could walk from ship to ship in Honolulu Harbor, and the channel between Lahaina and Lāna'i saw a peak of 429 ships anchored in 1846.

These rowdy newcomers caused much conflict. The newly Christian chiefs attempted to curtail drunkenness and to keep Hawaiian women from flocking to the ports, only to return home infected with disease. Some did not go home but sailed away, willingly or not, with the whalers. Thousands of young Hawaiian men chose to join a whaling crew and see the world, and some never returned.

Several factors contributed to the whaling industry's demise. Petroleum, first successfully pumped from the ground in 1859, lessened and eventually eliminated the need for whale oil to light America's lamps. The Civil War diverted ships to military use. Thirty-three ships were trapped and destroyed by Arctic ice floes in 1871. Their crews, including 500 Hawaiian seamen, managed to escape, but returned to the Islands destitute.

Farmers in Hawai'i, meanwhile, had been trying a variety of crops. They grew wheat, cotton, silkworms, and rice, and were particularly successful when the California Gold Rush created a market for fresh vegetables. That market died down after some of the miners discovered it was easier to make money farming than searching for gold.

Sugar takes the throne

For more than 100 years, sugar dominated Island life—economic, political, environmental, and social.

When the first major commercial planting took place on Kaua'i, in 1835, sugar was already a staple. The Hawaiians had grown it in rows alongside their **lo'i,** water-filled beds of kalo.

At first, sugar was just one of many crops post-contact farmers tried in their efforts to find something they could export to bring cash into Hawaii's isolated, debt-ridden economy. That first plantation's harvest in 1837 produced two tons of raw sugar, which sold for $200. In the next twenty years, a few more plantations got started, each struggling to survive.

The fledgling industry received a boost when the 1848 Māhele made it possible for planters to own land, and another when the Civil War cut off the North's supply of sugar grown in the South. When the Reciprocity Treaty of 1876 allowed Hawai'i's sugar and rice to enter the United States without tariffs, things really began to look up.

The Aiea Sugar Mill overlooked Pearl Harbor.

Sugar required water. It takes 500 gallons of water to produce a pound of sugar; a ton of sugar requires one million gallons. As the industry grew, planters channeled more and more water to Hawai'i's fertile but dry plains. They built an extensive system of irrigation ditches to carry water diverted from streams and dug deep wells to tap the aquifers formed over eons by rainwater seeping through the earth.

The old Hawaiians had been masters of irrigation, and the new haole planters borrowed their building techniques for the first ditches, hardened by the stomping of men's feet. The first significant sugar ditch built in this fashion was opened in 1856 by William Harrison Rice, founder of Lihuē Plantation on Kaua'i.

Such ditches were porous and lost water through seepage, so planters began lining the ditches with concrete. By the early 1900s, water flowed from the mountains through miles of ditches, flumes, and great tunnels blasted through mountains. Unlike the Hawaiians' irrigation systems, these ditches took water out of the streams and did not return it. By the 1920s, these systems diverted more than 100 million gallons a day, from more than 100 streams, making it possible for the sugar industry to flourish while impoverishing the natural land-scape through which the water would have flowed.

Forests were further devastated by cattle left to run wild after the initial kapu placed by Kamehameha I had populated the hills and valleys with livestock. Eventually, ranchers took over great tracts where their branded cattle ranged freely. Trampling and devouring native forests, cattle wreaked havoc on the exquisite biological jewel box that once had been harvested only with care and reverence by the Islands' original human inhabitants.

Settlers from many nations

Sugar also required labor, and meeting this need brought about Hawai'i's unusual ethnic mix. The Hawaiians were dying out, a people devastated by the changes that had descended upon their land. The planters looked elsewhere for workers.

They found them first among the peasants of China, Japan, and the Portuguese islands of Madeira and the Azores. In the early twentieth century, the sugar industry imported immigrants from Puerto Rico, Korea, Spain, and the Philippines.

Thousands of workers came, beginning with Chinese in 1852, many of whom planned to stay only for the life of a contract before returning rich to their home villages. While some did go home, others stayed, married Hawaiian women or brought picture brides from their homelands, remained on the plantation or struck out to begin their own small businesses.

Between 1877 and 1890, 55,000 immigrants arrived in Hawai'i. At the time of the overthrow, Hawaiians made up only about 45 percent of the population, while haole and Asians made up 55 percent.

Cutting cane by hand

At first, these laborers were segregated into plantation villages called **camps**. This made sense because the various nationalities were totally different in lifestyle and did not understand each other's languages, but it also suited the plantation oligarchy to keep them separate and ignorant of the fact that different groups were paid at different rates.

The plantations ran a patriarchal society, in which each person had his or her place, and many of their needs were met by their employer. Houses, schools, stores, medical care, food, and fuel were provided by the plantation. This system of "perquisites" discouraged labor organization; after all, if the boss owned everything, including one's home, rebellion seemed unwise if not impossible.

Gradually, despite the separate camps, this disparate group of people began to connect. At first, they developed a **pidgin**, a new language formed when speakers of different languages need to communicate.

Once pidgin emerges in a culture, it will be learned by adults as a second language. When children learn pidgin as their first language, and it becomes the mother tongue of the community, it is called a Creole. What is now known in Hawai'i as pidgin is technically named Hawai'i Creole English. This new language began to bring together a new kind of community, and though it has changed much over the decades, it still is the "carrier" of **local** culture.

As the years went by, children from the various nationalities went to school together, sports teams crossed racial boundaries, and people shared each other's food and holidays. Gradually, intermarriage began to link the ethnic groups. Many of the values these immigrants had brought from their rural homes were similar to those of their co-workers and also echoed the values of the cooperative subsistence culture of the Native Hawaiians.

An oligarchy rules

While the workers began to feel bonds that would in the 1920s cause them to label themselves "locals," Caucasians focused on their own connections. A small, inter-related oligarchy ran everything, clear in their own minds that they were superior to these non-Caucasian people they had brought in to work their fields. The haole elite, many of them missionary descendants, married each other's cousins and sisters, sat on each other's corporate boards, and promoted each other's businesses and politics.

Economically, Island life was dominated by the Big Five: Theo H. Davies, Alexander & Baldwin, Castle & Cooke, American Factors (Amfac), and C. Brewer. These companies had begun as agencies that coordinated business dealings for far-flung and isolated plantations, but by the early twentieth century, they pretty much ran the Islands.

Under this relatively benevolent patriarchy, the olig-archs established dozens of sugar plantations, ran cattle across vast upland ranches, and in the late 1800s, began to plant pineapple, which soon gained importance second only to sugar.

This social structure continued through the early 1900s, though the children of immigrant workers began to make small steps away from the fields and factories. Many of them took advantage of the opportunity to gain an education in the public high schools that began to open soon after Hawai'i became a territory.

Chugging along

Railroads once provided much of the transportation needed by Islanders and the crops that supported them.

Beginning with the first recorded locomotive run on Maui, in July 1879, trains chugged along tracks that crossed deep gulches on tall trestles, hauling sugar from field to harbor. Within the fields themselves, workers laid temporary tracks to take loads of harvested sugar to the permanent railways, which carried the harvest to mill or steamship. The trains also hauled mail, people, building materials and crops such as rice or sisal. According to the Hawai'ian Railway Society, 47 sugar plantations had private railway systems, each with from one to nine locomotives, and the military, too, had its own rail system. Trains ran on all the islands except Ni'ihau and Kaho'olawe.

Plantations established most of the railroads. On O'ahu, it was the railroad that made plantations possible. Benjamin Franklin Dillingham, a New Englander who arrived in Hawai'i in 1864, established the O'ahu Railway & Land Company, a narrow-gauge railway that made its first run in 1889. Dillingham's entrepreneurial spirit facilitated the development of both the sugar and pineapple industries on O'ahu, as well as the building of communities in Central O'ahu. Dillingham ran his rails around the then-undeveloped Pearl Harbor and created Hawai'i's first subdivision, Pearl City, along its banks.

Like other railroads in the Islands, Dillingham's declined as automobiles improved and trucks became available. World War II re-energized O'ahu's railroads when soldiers and war workers poured into the Islands. But by the 1950s, buses had taken over public transportation, and people wanted cars of their own. One by one, the trains stopped running, the equipment was sold or cut down for scrap, and the rails were recycled for fence posts and roof supports. The last railroad, like the first, was on Maui, where the final train ride took place in 1966.

Hawai'i's railroading days are pretty much finished, except for a short segment restored and operated by the Hawaiian Railway Society on O'ahu and tourist train rides on Maui and Kaua'i. As traffic jams make life in Hawai'i increasingly difficult (delaying the average motorist in Honolulu at least 20 hours a year), citizens and politicians often talk about the possibility of establishing some sort of light-rail system as an alternative to cars and buses. Too bad B. F. Dillingham is no longer with us.

The war changes everything

World War I had created economic problems as the big ships carrying cargo between Hawai'i and the Mainland were diverted for military use. Sugar shipping became difficult, and food shortages set in. But World War II had a much greater effect on Island life. The December 7, 1941, attack on Pearl Harbor shattered the peaceful plantation life of Hawai'i.

The territory had been preparing for war for several years with blackout practices, visits by the Pacific Fleet, and efforts to increase food production. Once the war began, strict martial law regulated every aspect of life. Everyone lived by stringent rules, made do with scarce supplies, and pitched in with volunteer civil defense efforts. School-children dug air-raid trenches on campus, and classes were canceled one day each week so students could work in fields and on farms to replace those who had gone to war. People collected scrap metal, bought War Bonds, and picked kiawe beans to feed livestock. Everyone carried a gas mask.

The early fear of an actual invasion was never realized, but Japanese submarines shelled places on the Neighbor Islands a few times. Though they caused little damage, some residents chose to send their children to the Mainland for the duration.

The Islands became a giant military training ground, with barbed wire guarding beaches and warriors training in cane fields and jungles. The military claimed great chunks of land for training, new bases, and POW camps, sometimes evicting longtime residents. Plantations plowed up sugar acreage and planted vegetables to feed the local population plus thousands of soldiers, sailors, Marines, and members of the Coast Guard.

On the Neighbor Islands, local communities often "adopted" the youngsters who returned from bloody battles in the Pacific to rest and recover. They entertained military men in private homes and at USO facilities that provided cookies and comfort, a place to write letters home and to dance with young local girls. In return, the visiting service-men put on rodeos and barbecues for their hosts and bought ice cream for kids who reminded them of their brothers and sisters back home. These personal contacts were the first many locals had ever had with Caucasians who were not in a position of power over them. They contributed to the changes the war brought to the social infrastructure.

Al Perry photo
*Marines Al Perry, Bob Fleishauer, and Bob Tierney
of the 4th Marine Division at Camp Maui.*

O'ahu streets swarmed with military men hungry for fun and female companionship. The Hotel Street district in Honolulu became a magnet, with long lines of uniformed man waiting to get into bars, brothels, and souvenir and tattoo shops. Because of the blackout, all of this action took place during daylight hours. While prostitution was not technically legal, it was tolerated; Hawai'i was filled with young, single men, often on their way to and from ferocious battles in the Pacific. Rationing meant tires and gasoline were hard to come by, so the military men, along with everyone else, traveled on the O'ahu Railway & Land Company's trains.

The nisei stand up

Another group of soldiers is remembered today for their grit and bravery in the face of racial discrimination.

When the war began, Hawai'i's population included 160,000 people of Japanese ancestry, totaling more than a third of the population. Many of them were **nisei**—or second generation—born in the United States, and therefore citizens. Older folks, fearing their loyalty would be questioned, focused on speaking English and getting rid of mementos from their homeland. Hawai'i's young men of Japanese ancestry were destined to prove their patriotism by bravery and sacrifice in the Armed Services.

Immediately after the attack on Pearl Harbor, young Americans of Japanese Ancestry (AJAs) who were members of the Territorial Guard went to their bases and were deployed to protect O'ahu. Several weeks later, they were discharged and their draft status changed to 4-C, or enemy aliens. Denied the opportunity to carry arms, the young men switched to hammers and shovels, volunteering for hard labor. This work apparently impressed the War Department, which commissioned 1,432 former Hawai'i National Guard members, all AJAs, as the 100th Infantry Battalion. The unit would fight in some of the heaviest combat in Italy. Their reputation in training on the Mainland encouraged the government to consider a segregated volunteer unit, and in February 1943, the 442nd Regimental Combat Team was activated. Ten thousand volunteered; 1,686 were sent to the Mainland for training and then to join the 100th Battalion in Europe. The 442nd Regimental Combat team became the most decorated unit in U.S. history for its size and length of service. Meanwhile, others in the Military Intelligence Service were providing invaluable information and earning medals of their own as translators.

The AJA soldiers lived and died by their motto, Go for Broke, meaning to gamble everything. As they saved lives and gave their own, their loyalty to the United States was unquestionable.

Back home, their relatives were busy proving their loyalty by their work for the war effort. Unlike the Mainland, where about 120,000 AJAs were interned, fewer than 1,500 of Hawai'i's Japanese Americans were detained on suspicion of disloyalty.

Hawai'i's Japanese Americans escaped internment in greater numbers partly because of their longtime integration into the Hawai'i community, but also because sheer numbers made it impossible to ship or house them in internment centers. They were a major segment of Hawai'i's work force, and about half of Honolulu's retail businesses were run by Japanese Americans. They were essential to the continued functioning of the Islands' economy.

In addition, writer and filmmaker Tom Coffman says, a multi-ethnic Council for Interracial Unity that formed in 1939 developed lines of communication to be used in the event of a war between the United States and Japan. When the war started, members of the Council—and organizations that they launched—worked to calm fears, promote demonstrations of patriotism, and speak out against mass internment.

A key aspect of their work was to argue for the right to serve the country. They helped bring about the mass mobilization of young men for service in the soon-to-be-famed 442nd Regimental Combat Team.

The infrastructure of relationships that these groups organized became the political structure that forged great changes in the post-war governance of Hawai'i. In the long run, Coffman says, the war put Hawai'i ethnic groups on more equal footing and laid the groundwork for Hawai'i to become the 50th State.

Ironically, while Hawai'i's Americans of Japanese ancestry spent their war years working to prove their loyalty, the only person convicted of espionage in Hawai'i during the war was a German alien.

Young nisei men return from fighting in World War II.

If the powers that ran the Islands expected the young men who had gone to war to return submissively to the cane fields after the war, they were in for a surprise.

It was a classic case of "How you gonna keep 'em down on the farm after they've seen Paree." The nisei veterans took advantage of their GI Bill benefits, went back to school, and emerged with law degrees and other credentials that allowed them to enter the middle class and, within years, to dominate Island politics. In 1954, World War II veterans led the Democratic takeover of the Territorial Legislature, dislodging the Republican oligarchy that had run the Islands for decades.

Meanwhile, back on the farm

The end of the war meant intensive labor organization. Efforts had been suspended during the war, when all jobs and wages were frozen, and it would have seemed unpatriotic to challenge the existing power structure.

Once martial law was lifted in 1944, however, union organizers got to work. They broke the back of the "perquisite" system in 1946 with the first Territory-wide sugar strike. Workers sought higher wages, rather than plantation-provided homes in camps where many of the old and relatively primitive houses lacked indoor plumbing.

The shipping strike of 1949 is the best remembered of all strikes in Hawai'i history. Longshoremen struck over a wage increase, leaving full ships tied up in the harbors and stopping harvests in the cane fields as raw sugar piled up in local warehouses.

When the strike finally ended 177 days later, millions of dollars had been lost, businesses had gone bankrupt, and the entire Territory had suffered. For the rest of the century, rumors of a dock strike would send consumers scurrying to stock up on rice and toilet paper.

Statehood + jets = tourism

This formula changed Hawai'i irrevocably. Statehood, in 1959, raised awareness on the Mainland of this tiny, exotic piece of the United States, and jets cut travel time in half.

While O'ahu's population had continued to grow, nearly doubling between 1940 and 1960, the Neighbor Island economies were stagnating. Their populations dropped as the sugar industry became more mechanized and needed fewer laborers. The brightest of Hawai'i's young people went off to college on the Mainland and never returned. In 1957, for example, only 13 of 166 Maui High School seniors planned to remain on Maui following graduation.

The answer seemed to be to develop a new industry. There always had been visitors, beginning with intrepid travelers like Isabella Bird and Mark Twain in the 1800s, and Waikīkī had seen its first hotels built in the late 1800s and early 1900s. In 1903, the Territorial Legislature made its first appropriation for visitor promotion. In 1921, the first year records were kept, 9,400 vacationers visited. That same year, the dredging of Waikīkī began, and by 1928, the streams that had fed its wetlands all had been diverted into the Ala Wai Canal.

The ancient playground of the ali'i was to become the commercial image of Hawai'i, projected around the world to attract tourists. Matson Navigation Company lured elite passengers for its ocean liners with the promise of an elegant place to stay, building the Royal Hawaiian Hotel in 1927. Each year, the number of visitors grew.

The war slowed things down but also set the stage for postwar growth by exposing thousands of Mainland military people to Hawai'i's beauty. Hawai'i has spent billions reinforcing its romantic image, and the industry has grown and brought prosperity.

Now, with more than seven million visitors a year, the state's tourist industry seems to be hostage to its own success. People who love to visit Hawai'i often fantasize about living here, and many have made the move. Island residents are concerned about burgeoning population growth, continuing land development, and increasing urbanization.

As far back as the late '60s, when the big push was on to improve opportunities for the Islands' young people, some warned that unchecked development could seriously degrade Hawai'i's quality of life. The current water shortages, traffic jams, and housing crunch demonstrate that those warnings were justified. Many argue for sustainable growth that would preserve the local lifestyle, values, and environment and point out that these will not survive in an economy that relies on low-wage service jobs while real estate prices soar.

'Āina: that which feeds us

Moving into the twenty-first century, Islanders fretted about the loss of agricultural lands, as the traditional crops faced challenges that ended sugar and pineapple cultivation in many places. The good news: With increased awareness and appreciation for the importance of green space and the need to feed and power the Islands, entrepreneurs and landowners are raising everything from goats to gourmet greens, and community planning sessions clearly indicate that Hawai'i's people want to make the Islands as sustainable as possible.

In late 2007, only two sugar plantations remain in the Islands. Hawaiian Commercial & Sugar Company on Maui and Gay & Robinson on Kaua'i struggle to remain profitable and protect from development thousands of acres kept green by agriculture.

The future of sugar, and of the vast fields that cover otherwise dusty plains, face many pressures: competition from foreign producers whose governments subsidize their crops, the high cost of wages for the world's best-paid agricultural workers, and the continual effort to maintain healthy crops in a system of monoculture that is inherently unnatural.

Why not simply plow the fields and plant other crops? Why do the Hawaiian Islands not feed themselves, but import fruit and vegetables from afar? These are questions with no simple answers. In fact, diversified agriculture is a growing facet of the Hawai'i economy, and those who want to support Island farmers can do so by buying locally grown food in stores or at farmers markets. Still, far-away farms produce vast quantities of food at prices local growers cannot match after dealing with the high costs of land, water, and labor. Many local farmers focus on specialty or gourmet crops that will attract discriminating shoppers and fine restaurants offering fresh "Hawai'i Regional Cuisine."

Even if farmers could solve problems of production and distribution, there is far more land available than would be needed simply to feed the state's population. The entire Hawai'i market could be supplied with about 10,000 acres' worth of crops. Statewide, 1.9 million acres are zoned for agricultural use.

As always, in this place where nearly anything grows, finding something that can be grown for profit means finding something that can be sent somewhere else. On these Islands, which are farther from anywhere than any- where else on earth, farmers have yet to find a way to replace the old commodity crops of sugar and pineapple, and for the time being, at least, the artificial structures set up more than a century ago to support these crops remain in place to keep vast sections of Island land green.

Maui's sugar industry faces much controversy among both newcomers and kama'āina. Kaua'i sugar operations do not face the same problems. Cane smoke on that island tends to blow out to sea, and the abundant water flowing from Mount Wai'ale'ale easily irrigates Gay & Robinson's 7,400 acres of cane.

On Maui, however, newcomers often complain of the cane smoke that clouds their South Maui homes. Enormous fires set to burn off the "rubbish," leaving bare cane for harvest, send giant plumes of smoke into the sky. The trade winds blow this smoke to the bustling new communities on the south shore.

The sugar industry is not about to stop the practice, despite protests. The industry has tried for years to come up with alternative harvesting methods but has yet to find anything that will work. Giant rocks and long stalks of cane lying flat along the ground make it impossible to mow cane like a vast lawn. Sugar relies on burning in order to harvest efficiently.

On the positive side, the fields receive minimal herbicides, and irrigation pipe that burns in the fires breaks down to simple carbon dioxide and water, so at least the smoke is not contaminated by chemicals—it's just plain old ash, with some red Maui dirt mixed in. Nothing that you'd choose to breathe but not as bad as some people fear.

Water worries

Many residents have other concerns about the vast acres of cane on the Central Maui isthmus. This area is naturally dry and sandy, and cane flourishes here only because of irrigation with water from the rainy slopes of East Maui. And even on the islands where sugar plantations no longer exist, water issues are critical and controversial.

The sugar industry originally took hold because of water piped in from rainy areas. In the late twentieth century, challenges to the use of water from windward streams for sugarcane contributed to the closing of some plantations as residential populations grew, and as the state claimed ownership and control of water.

Beginning in the 1870s, the plantation water systems tapped streams that used to flow down natural water courses to irrigate Hawaiian lo'i. Some of the original leases for tapping the streams required that the plantations' taking of water not impinge on the rights of other users. Over the years, that requirement often was disregarded. The plantation ditches permanently removed water from the stream and channeled it away from the watershed, rather than returning it to the stream as Hawaiian irrigation systems had done. Streams dried up as the ditches diverted their waters, as forest destruction allowed rain to run off rather than soak in and restore the watershed, and as wells pumped out groundwater that would have helped replenish stream flow.

EMI photo
An East Maui Irrigation Company ditch

In addition to leaving kalo growers with no water, the dry stream beds threaten the existence of native species that, like the salmon of America's Northwest, need to migrate up and down the stream as part of their life cycle.

The old Hawaiians, with their word for wealth (waiwai) simply a repetition of their word for water, were wiser than many moderns in their understanding of humanity's dependence on nature, and on the essential value of plain old water.

While some areas of the Islands today depend on the old irrigation systems, and others on well water from aquifers deep beneath the mountains, nearly all of Hawai'i faces water shortages, and everyone who lives here should understand that and act accordingly to conserve this most important resource.

Hala kahiki: the foreign hala

If sugar was "king" of plantation Hawai'i, pineapple was "prince." No one knows for sure when or how pineapple arrived in Hawai'i—Captain Cook's botanists did not record it among the many other plants they reported in 1778. By 1813, however, it was present in the Honolulu gardens of Don Francisco de Paula y Marín, who is usually credited with introducing the fruit. Pineapple's Hawaiian name is "hala kahiki," or "foreign pandanus," because its fruit looks like the fruit of the hala, the leggy native pandanus whose straplike leaves are used to make lau hala mats. Pineapple was plentiful in the Islands by the mid-1800s, and a number of farmers established commercial plantings, with varying success.

James D. Dole, probably the most important man in the development of Hawai'i's pineapple industry, acquired 61 acres in Wahiawā on O'ahu in 1900. Realizing that the only way to market this fruit on a national level was to can it, Dole built a cannery. An engineer working for him, Henry Ginaca, invented a machine that could peel, core, and cut the fruit at the speed of 80 to 100 pineapples per minute. By

1915, Dole's Hawaiian Pineapple Company had become Hawai'i's second largest industry.

Pineapple pickers

In 1922, Dole bought the nearly deserted island of Lāna'i for $1.1 million and converted it to the largest pineapple plantation in the world, with 20,000 acres in fruit. Eventually, the "Pineapple Island" supplied nearly 75 percent of the world's pineapple. Farmers on other islands also planted the crop, and by 1930, eight canneries were packing nine million cases of pineapple a year.

The Great Depression hit pineapple hard. Sugar was a staple; although prices dropped, sugar continued to sell. Canned pineapple, however, was a luxury for most consumers, and the warehouses were full. Canning was curtailed and workers were laid off. Farmers invited the public to help themselves as fruit began to rot in the fields. James Dole, short of funds, lost control of Hawaiian Pineapple to Castle & Cooke.

Pineapple workers organized after World War II, conducting their first strike in 1947. The industry continued to grow through the '50s but began to decline in the mid-1960s. Only three canneries remained by the 1970s, and in the 1980s the three major producers, Dole, Del Monte, and Maui Pineapple Company, began to focus on the sale of fresh fruit. By the 1990s, foreign competition had made pineapple unprofitable, and Lāna'i's new owner built two golf courses and two luxury hotels, now the island's economic engine.

Pineapple managed to survive into the twenty-first century only on Maui and O'ahu. In 2006, Del Monte Fresh Produce (Hawai'i) Inc. suddenly ceased operations on O'ahu, citing low production and depressed prices. This left 551 employees out of work, 5,100 acres of fruit unharvested, and only Dole Food Company growing "pine" on O'ahu. In 2007, Maui Land & Pineapple Company shut down "solid-pack" fruit-canning operations at its Kahului cannery, the last in the Islands, saying huge financial losses on the canned-fruit operation spurred the shutdown. The company now specializes in growing fresh pineapple and developing land.

Henry Baldwin digs a ditch

The story of Henry Perrine Baldwin has all the ingredients of popular fiction: a humble, hard-working hero who must overcome many obstacles to reach his goal, a trusty side-kick, a plucky heroine, and a villain lurking in the wings. Of course, the sugar pioneers on each island have their own stories, but Baldwin's has some special qualities. He led construction of sugar's first major irrigation system and co-created a corporation that still grows cane and plays a role in Island business today.

Henry was born in 1842 in the seaside town of Lahaina, Maui, the son of missionaries Dwight and Charlotte Fowler Baldwin. He grew up in the house that today is the oldest existing building on Maui, the Baldwin Home Museum on Front Street. His father was Maui's only doctor, and his mother reared six children and played hostess to Lahaina characters ranging from ship captains to wandering artists. One imagines young Henry as barefoot and brown, running errands for his father or playing in the dusty streets. He grew up familiar with Hawai'i and its language, pious in his Christianity, and as educated as a young man could be far from the great schools of his parents' East Coast home.

When Henry was just a year old, another missionary family moved to town. Their son Samuel Alexander had been born in a grass house on Kaua'i in 1836. Samuel's father, William Alexander, headed the Lahainaluna School.

Henry and Samuel both attended Punahou School in Honolulu and as young men went to work on early sugar plantations. In 1869, the two decided to go into business for themselves. They bought 12 acres of land below Makawao, in Upcountry Maui, and began growing sugar cane on this first piece of what would become a great sugar empire. Perhaps fitting for the beginning of an empire, their families also were joined by marriage in 1870, when Henry married Samuel's sister Emily.

Cameron Family photo
Henry P. Baldwin

Life was not easy for the young farmers. Henry spent most of his days in the saddle. Drought was a continual problem for their water-thirsty crop. By 1876, Alexander and Baldwin and their partners had decided to undertake an ambitious project with long-lasting consequences for their own lives and for much of the island of Maui. They would dig a water ditch to irrigate 2,000 to 3,000 acres of land in Ha'ikū and on the lower western slopes of Haleakalā.

The ditch would begin in the jungles of East Maui, where the trade winds blow rain against the side of the mountain, creating an abundance of water that flows in streams to the sea. For 17 miles, the ditch would meander down gulches and over hillsides, collecting water and carrying it to the dry lands where Alexander and Baldwin already were expanding their plantings.

The partners obtained a license from the Kingdom of Hawai'i to tap this water, which required that they complete construction of the ditch within two years. If they did not finish the job in the time allotted, they would forfeit all rights to the ditch and the water.

The deadline was given added urgency by the fact that King Kalākaua's gambling buddy, California financier Claus Spreckels, also was in the sugar business on Maui, and would be only too happy to take over the missionary boys' half-finished job. With that possibility as extra incentive, the partners swung into action on the first great irrigation ditch project in Hawai'i.

Alexander did the detailed planning for the project. Baldwin personally supervised its construction, with a gang of men sometimes numbering 200 employed in the work. The company provided food, shelter, and tools, cutting roads through the woods to bring in supplies. They hauled in heavy timbers for flumes and blasted tunnels through rock. Pipe fitters from San Francisco riveted great sheets of iron into huge lengths to cross deep ravines.

For Henry, this was a particularly daunting project. In March 1876, while he was demonstrating the unevenness of the gap between the rollers that crushed cane in his sugar mill, his fingers were caught in the opening. The machinery was still on, and Henry Baldwin's right arm was pulled in and crushed to the elbow.

A rider galloped down to Wailuku to summon the

doctor, who returned to amputate Henry's arm. As darkness descended, someone finally had to tell Emily Baldwin why her husband, recovering in a home near the sugar mill, was not coming home that night. First thing the next morning, Emily—eight and one-half months pregnant—climbed onto a horse and went to be with her injured husband.

Henry Baldwin was a determined man. Soon, he had taught himself to write, ride, and even play the organ with his left hand. An accomplished player since childhood, he was the faithful Sunday organist at his church in Makawao for 40 years.

With Alexander away on a trip to the Mainland, it fell to Henry to manage the construction of the great ditch, even when he was so weak from his injury that he sometimes had to ride off to a secluded area to lie down for a while.

The greatest challenge came when it was time to cross Māliko Gulch, 300 feet deep and 800 feet wide, its steep sides made of solid rock. To do this required that a pipe 24 inches in diameter be attached to the side of the gulch, run across the bottom of the gulch, and back up the other side. Workers on the project had trouble believing that water could actually be made to travel uphill when the grade at the exit was below that at the intake. They were even more doubtful about the idea of attaching the pipe to the side of the gulch. And when informed that they would have to lower themselves over the cliff and into the deep ravine, they simply refused.

So Baldwin clutched a rope with his legs and his single arm and rappelled the 300 feet into the gulch. Shamed by their leader's courage, the men dutifully followed. Baldwin repeated this feat each day until the ravine had been crossed. The partners made their deadline, with time to spare.

More irrigation ditches would tap the streams of East Maui in years to come (parts of the system can be seen by travelers on the Hana Highway), and this water supply made possible not only the cultivation of sugar but the growth of Upcountry as a population center. The massive project provided an example that planters on other islands soon followed. And it set Alexander and Baldwin on a path to great success. Eventually, they took over the Hawaiian Commercial & Sugar Company established by their rival, Claus Spreckels. Today, HC&S is an amalgamation of various smaller plantations the partners created, and one of only two surviving sugar plantations in the Islands. Alexander & Baldwin Inc. has grown into a $1.5 billion corporation, quite an improvement from the days when Sam Alexander and Henry Baldwin struggled to keep their sugar alive through another dry summer season.

EMI photo

Irrigation ditch carries water to thirsty sugar fields

The Islands Today

The Big Who?

Whatever happened to the Big Five? A few decades ago, it was possible to point with certainty to the most powerful entities in Hawai'i.

But the five companies that once controlled much of what transpired in Hawai'i are no longer the powers that be. Amfac, C. Brewer & Company, and Theo H. Davies have disappeared from the Island scene, their assets sold and their influence gone. Castle & Cooke evolved into the Dole Food Company and operates in Hawai'i mostly as a real estate developer and property manager. Only Alexander & Baldwin still does big business in the Islands, and it no longer wields the political clout it did in the early years of the past century.

Business reporter Howard Dicus, an astute observer of the local scene, suggests that a whole new set of players comprise the Big Five for our time. Dicus lists the banks, which can make or break a business by lending decisions; the unions, much more powerful than those on the Mainland; the military, which generates many jobs; environmentalists, whose passion to protect the natural world is shared by many in public and private life; and Native Hawaiian activists, who have revived concepts of aloha, 'ohana, pono behavior, and protecting the 'āina, all now widely accepted (and, one hopes, practiced) in the political, social, and business worlds.

Of course, modern Hawai'i is so strongly connected to the outside world that probably no one will ever wield the all-encompassing power those big companies did a hundred years ago. It's hard to imagine any group of entities as intertwined and cohesive as the big companies of the past in this free-flowing world. The forces that influence Hawai'i destiny today include those from faraway places, such as the economic impact of Asian industries and relatively anonymous arrivals like the super-rich who choose Hawai'i as a second home or a place to invest their millions.

One major new influence is a returned kama'āina: Steve Case, founder of America Online. Born into a family who have lived in Hawai'i for several generations, Case bought into Maui Land & Pineapple Company (where he is majority stockholder) and is 100 percent owner of Grove Farm Company on Kaua'i. These companies are the second-largest private landowners on their respective islands, giving Case considerable clout in determining future development.

Green power

As the world agricultural economy makes it harder for Hawai'i food producers to survive, the world energy economy seems to favor a move to bioenergy crops. Major landowners across the state are exploring crops that could be turned into either ethanol or biodiesel. While it's not clear yet if any of these crops make economic sense, the rising financial and political costs of oil dependence have attracted the interest of international energy entrepreneurs to Hawai'i. If nothing else, we know the Islands can grow sugar, the feed source for the ethanol that powers Brazil.

Hawai'i already is an energy leader, producing about 7 percent of its energy from renewable sources, compared to the 2 percent national average. Solar panels heat water on thousands of roofs statewide, many purchased with the help of tax credits and zero- and low-interest loans. Ordinary trash is turned into renewable energy on O'ahu, geothermal energy is tapped in Puna on Hawai'i Island, and wind is captured by towers on Maui and Hawai'i. Both HC&S and Gay & Robinson burn bagasse, the fibrous material left after cane juice is removed, converting each ton of the cane trash into steam power equivalent to a barrel of oil. And on Maui, the pioneering Pacific Biodiesel operation has perfected the science of turning used restaurant grease into automobile fuel that makes car exhaust smell like French fries.

The state government encourages these efforts; even with the amount of alternate energy now feeding the grid, Hawai'i is still highly dependent on imported oil. State laws require that gas now contain 10 percent ethanol and that, by 2020, 20 percent of the state's energy be derived from renewable sources.

Wind towers capture energy on a West Maui ridge.

Hawai'i is only the second state in the country to commit to reducing greenhouse gases, modeling its goals on those set by the Kyoto Protocol. The state sweetens these requirements by offering tax credits to producers, an offer of great interest to power companies, sugar producers, farmers looking for future crops, and venture capitalists seeking investments.

How these isolated Islands will fare as petroleum grows

ever more expensive is on a lot of minds these days, and many efforts are under way to tap Hawai'i's abundant natural resources. I'm pinning my hopes on the development of efficient bioenergy crops. If they succeed, the green fields of growing things that have made Hawai'i a place of fertile beauty for many centuries will continue to flourish into the future.

The military

The military is big business in Hawai'i. The U.S. armed forces have a long history here and generally good relations with a community well aware that the military, with expenditures of $5.6 billion in 2005, is the state's second major source of revenue, eclipsed only by tourism.

The U.S. military presence in Hawai'i goes back well over a hundred years, to the days when Pearl Harbor's strategic importance was first recognized. The right to use the harbor was an important bargaining point when the kingdom sought to sell its agricultural products to the United States. The "Bayonet Constitution" of 1887 ceded exclusive use of the harbor to the United States in exchange for dropping the tariff on sugar.

A few years later, U.S. Marines came ashore to provide a silent but effective backup for the coup that overthrew the Hawaiian monarchy. Just days after the Hawaiian Islands were officially annexed as a U.S. Territory in 1898, a small Army garrison set up camp at the foot of Diamond Head. In 1902, the coral reef at the mouth of Pearl Harbor was dredged, and ancient ponds and traps once used to harvest the harbor's rich fisheries were destroyed.

U.S. involvement in World War II began with the infamous attack on Pearl Harbor as the Japanese sought to cripple the Pacific Fleet. While it was American ships that drew fire that day, it seems likely that Japan would have attacked Hawai'i in any case. If the military had not been here to defend them, the Islands' central position, plus that fabulous harbor, would have made them ideal stepping stones for Japanese aggression.

Today's Islanders have mixed views on the military presence. Some see it as vital to U.S. security and to the state's economy. Some Hawaiian rights activists think the military is part of an illegal occupation. And many Islanders are concerned about the environmental damages caused by some military activities.

Statewide, the military controls some 240,000 acres, including 22.4 percent of the land on O'ahu. Hawai'i is headquarters for the U.S. Pacific Command, and every branch is represented here. The largest concentration is on O'ahu, where the Commander in Chief of the Pacific Fleet is stationed at Pearl Harbor, military personnel are a visible and economically powerful presence, and Tripler Army Medical Center provides health care for thousands. Pearl Harbor is the state's largest industrial employer; when a federal base closure panel considered shutting down the Pearl Harbor Naval Shipyard in 2005, threatening some 5,000 jobs, Hawai'i officials flew to Washington, D.C., to argue successfully for the shipyard's future.

Other major O'ahu facilities include the Marine Corps Base Hawai'i in Kāne'ohe, Schofield Barracks, Hickam Air Force Base, Fort Shafter, the Mākua Military Reservation, and the Coast Guard base on Sand Island.

Military influence extends far beyond O'ahu. The Barking Sands Pacific Missile Range Hawaii is Kaua'i's second largest employer and its largest high-tech facility, performing six to eight major missile tests a year from a 7-mile stretch on the west coast of the island. On Hawai'i Island, the Pōhakuloa Training Area is the largest U.S.-owned training area in the state. On Maui, the military is somewhat less visible than on the other main islands, but the Air Force Optical Tracking Station atop Haleakalā and the supercomputer at the Maui Research & Technology Park are key installations.

The Chamber of Commerce of Hawai'i and many in the business community support the military presence because of its economic input, as well as its importance in national defense. Ongoing programs to privatize the construction, renovation, and operation of military housing will invest about $3 billion over the next decade, which is expected to help stabilize the economy in the event of a downturn. Federal funding for research and development has contributed to growth of the local high-technology industry. The Coast Guard is particularly helpful in an island state; in 2006, the Chamber reports, the Coast Guard conducted 1,200 search-and-rescue missions and saved 409 lives.

Organizations like DMZ Hawaii/Aloha 'Āina focus on the downside of military presence. Many people are concerned about the military taking vast stretches of land and the environmental effects of military training on places like Mākua Valley on West O'ahu and the Pōhakuloa Training area on the Big Island. Fires sparked by training exercises have destroyed native plants and threatened archaeological sites, chemical and conventional weapons have been discarded offshore, and environmental pollutants from unexploded ordnance to heavy metals threaten human health.

Conflicts in recent years have included protests against sonar testing that harms marine mammals and the 2005 occupation of the office of the University of Hawai'i president. The occupation forced the Board of Regents to delay agreement on a Navy plan to establish a University Affiliated Research Center to conduct weapons-related research, though the delay was temporary, and the regents have since approved the center. As is often the case, opponents of such projects as the establishment of a Stryker Brigade Combat Team at Schofield are matched by those who support the expansion of the military presence because of its economic value to the Islands.

With such an overwhelming economic influence and the Islands' continued strategic value, the U.S. military will not leave Hawai'i any time soon. But perhaps the protests by citizens can make the military slow down and proceed with more care than it has in the past. In late 2006, a federal appellate court found that the Army had violated environmental laws by not considering all alternatives to establishing a Stryker Combat Brigade in Hawai'i, stalling the project and perhaps setting a precedent for future military activities.

What about the Hawaiians?

While settlers from many lands prospered in Hawai'i, the native people of the Islands continued to suffer. David Malo, the most famous of the early Lahainaluna Seminary scholars, had predicted an overwhelming tide when "clever men from the big countries" would arrive to devour Hawai'i, knowing that "our people are few in number and our country is small."

Suffering innumerable personal losses from imported illnesses that killed thousands and left others sterile, bereft of their religion, their land, and their kingdom, Hawaiians did indeed face an overwhelming tide of foreign invasion.

Statistics reflect the trauma of the past 200 years: Hawaiians have high rates of illness, incarceration, substance abuse, and welfare dependence, among other signals of distress. Though many individual Native Hawaiians thrive and succeed, Hawaiian people as a whole suffer from a sort of cultural post-traumatic stress disorder.

There is hope, however, that in time these wounds to the Hawaiian spirit will heal. The image held both by Hawaiians and others of the native culture began to change in the 1970s. It was a time when people across the country were seeking their roots, learning about their own ethnic backgrounds and ancestry. The native people of Hawai'i also began to look more closely at their history and to take increased pride in their culture.

Among the concepts these Hawaiians rediscovered was that of **aloha 'āina**, or love for the land. Kaho'olawe, an island off Maui's southwest coast, had served as a bombing target for the U.S. military since the beginning of World War II. It became a rallying point. As Hawaiians considered the damage that alienation from their own land had done to their people, the plight of Kaho'olawe came to symbolize the need to reconnect with and protect the 'āina.

In January 1976, a group of nine men and women landed on the island. When the Coast Guard arrived with orders to remove the group, two of the men were out of sight, and chose not to show themselves. Walter Ritte and Noa Emmett Aluli spent two days on a spiritual sojourn that became a catalyst and a turning point for Hawai'i.

Many landings took place after this first one, and the activists formed the **Protect Kaho'olawe 'Ohana**. The Navy began to allow groups access to the island for Hawaiian religious ceremonies—and each time there were people on the island, whether authorized or not, the bombing stopped. An archaeological survey confirmed that there were many valuable sites, and the entire island was found to be eligible for the National Register of Historic Places. There were protests, arrests, and trials, and some protestors served time in jail. Two men, George Helm (one of the 'Ohana's founders) and Kimo Mitchell, were lost at sea, apparently while trying to paddle surfboards back to Maui.

A civil lawsuit and several years of struggle resulted in a 1980 consent decree between the Navy and the 'Ohana. The consent decree allowed limited access for restricted purposes and required an archaeological survey and control of the wild goats that were devastating what remained of the island's plant life. Bombing stopped in 1990, and in 1994 the island was returned to the State of Hawai'i, and its cleanup and restoration began.

The island is now controlled by the Kaho'olawe Island Reserve Commission. By state law, the Kaho'olawe Island Reserve is to be managed in trust until such time and circumstances as a sovereign Native Hawaiian entity is recognized by the federal and state governments. The island may be used only for noncommercial cultural, scientific, and educational purposes.

Dave DeLeon photo

The late Uncle Harry Mitchell examines artifacts on Kahoʻolawe.
His son Kimo was lost at sea during efforts to stop bombing.

Another important turning point was the construction of *Hōkūleʻa*. This Hawaiian sailing canoe was built by the Polynesian Voyaging Society, a group determined to prove that the people who originally settled these Islands had sailed across the Pacific from other islands in Polynesia.

Despite the clear similarities in language, culture, and physical characteristics between the people of Hawaiʻi and of other islands such as Tahiti, Tonga, and Sāmoa, it seemed incredible to think that people in tiny canoes could have made the journey between far-flung islands so long ago. Some thought that perhaps the Hawaiians had simply drifted with the trade winds from South America.

When *Hōkūleʻa* left Hawaiʻi in 1976 and sailed to Tahiti without modern instrumentation, it proved to the world that indeed traditional navigational techniques could be used to sail great distances between islands. Remarkably, the navigator on this journey was a man from Micronesia—

there was no one left in Hawai'i who knew the skills required. And though Mau Piailug was far from his home waters, he was able to use his knowledge of the sky, the sea, and the wind to direct *Hōkūle'a* to its destination.

The voyage inspired people all over the Pacific to revive their canoe-based cultures, and sparked a series of journeys that connected the peoples whose ancestors once shared these seas.

This accomplishment brought renewed pride to Native Hawaiians, contributing to the **Hawaiian Renaissance** of culture and language that had begun in the early '70s thanks largely to Hawaiian musicians like Gabby Pahinui. Today, thousands of Islanders paddle with canoe clubs. Others practice dance and chant that recorded the history and legends of their people in pre-contact days. Hawaiian music is more vibrant than ever, as musicians bring back treasured songs from the past and create new ones.

One of the most significant revivals is that of the Hawaiian language itself. Beginning in the 1980s, educators concerned about this dying language realized that the best way to ensure its survival was to teach it to children in their early years, when they are most able to absorb language.

Using a model developed in New Zealand, they founded the **'Aha Pūnana Leo** (language nest) schools, in which preschoolers are immersed in an environment of spoken Hawaiian. Some Pūnana Leo students continue in Hawaiian-language programs in public schools through high school. Today, the revival of the language has reached the top of the academic world. In 2007, the University of Hawai'i-Hilo began offering a doctorate degree in Hawaiian and indigenous language and culture revitalization. The nation's first doctorate in an indigenous language, the degree is offered by the College of Hawaiian Language, which operates entirely in Hawaiian.

 Locals Know: *The word* **kanaka** *was sometimes used derisively to refer to Hawaiians by malihini of an earlier time, but it has been proudly reclaimed by modern Hawaiians. Among its meanings are*

"human being, man, mankind, person." Adding the prefix "ho'o" creates ho'okanaka: "manly, human, courageous." Today, many Native Hawaiians refer to themselves as **kanaka maoli***, meaning a person who is "native" or "indigenous."*

Sovereignty

You have arrived in Hawai'i at a very interesting time. A century after their kingdom was overthrown, the Hawaiian people began to organize politically to regain **sovereignty**. What this will mean has long been debated, and there are many ideas about how the Hawaiian people might regain control of their destiny as a nation. A leading group in the movement, Ka Lāhui Hawai'i, defines sovereignty as "the ability of a people who share a common culture, religion, language, value system, and land base to exercise control over their lands and lives, independent of other nations."

What does this portend for the future of Hawai'i, its residents, and its connection to the United States? No one knows at this point. Newcomers interested in learning more about this complex issue can do so by reading some of the books listed on the website of the Office of Hawaiian Affairs, www.oha.org, which includes books by several of the most influential leaders of the sovereignty movement. Another resource is at www.HawaiianKingdom.info. It links to a variety of interesting local sites and includes the text of many documents important to the history and politics of Hawai'i.

As the debate continues, various organizations and issues make the headlines on a regular basis. Here are a few of the names you are likely to run across:

The Office of Hawaiian Affairs is a semi-autonomous state body with a Board of Trustees elected by the state's registered voters. OHA grew out of the Constitutional Convention of 1978, a time when the Hawaiian people had begun to stand up to fight for the preservation of their lands and culture. OHA is funded by a share of the revenues of the ceded lands, the crown and government lands of the

Kingdom of Hawai'i that were ceded first to the Republic of Hawai'i and then to the United States. OHA has programs to promote Hawaiians' economic development, housing, education, and governance. Its Kau Inoa project is collecting a list of people of Hawaiian ancestry willing to participate in the process of establishing a new Native Hawaiian government.

The Department of Hawaiian Home Lands is the state agency that administers the Hawaiian Home Lands program and trust created by legislation pushed though Congress by Hawai'i Representative Prince Jonah Kuhiō in 1921. Its mission is to place eligible Hawaiians on 203,500 acres of the 1.8 million acres of ceded lands. Sounds like a great idea, but the lands were sadly mismanaged for many years, and many Hawaiians languished on a long list of candidates for homestead land, often dying before they reached the top of the list. Meanwhile, ranchers, the U.S. military, and others leased land at a fraction of its value. The administration of Governor Linda Lingle made it a goal to get people on the land, and the department has opened several Hawaiian Home Lands housing developments in recent years.

The Kamehameha Schools/Bishop Estate: The schools were founded by the will of Bernice Pauahi Bishop, great-granddaughter of Kamehameha I. The School for Boys was established in 1887 in Honolulu, and the School for Girls opened in 1894. In 1965, the school became co-ed. There are now also campuses on Maui and Hawai'i Island. In addition to the K-12 schools, Kamehameha operates preschools statewide, as well as outreach and scholarship programs. The schools subsidize the costs of education, using the revenues of the Bishop Estate, the largest private landowner in Hawai'i. The schools also give preference to "Hawaiians of pure or part aboriginal blood," as specified in Princess Pauahi's will. This has caused some controversy and even legal challenges. Some say this policy is racist, while others point to the catastrophe and oppression that overwhelmed the Hawaiian population and say the princess had a right to leave her private fortune, inherited from royal ancestors, for the benefit of her people.

Princess Bernice Pauahi Bishop

What's in a word?

Shakespeare's question is particularly important in Hawai'i, where language traditionally carries power, and a strong local culture claims ownership of certain words and phrases.

Take, for example, that word "local." You'll hear it used often, but if you have moved here, it is better not to use it when referring to yourself. In Hawai'i, the word "local" does not mean people who happen to live here. In this context, there are a variety of ways to define the word.

Local might mean working-class people of color (except that Portuguese count despite their European origin, because of their plantation background). It might mean someone born here, or someone who grew up in Hawai'i. Some people think it applies to anyone with a certain state of mind, living a certain kind of lifestyle. Others insist that the concept of being "Hawaiian at heart" simply does not apply to those of us who are transplants from the Mainland.

This whole thing, clearly, is another version of political correctness—local style!

Many characteristics of the local lifestyle are based on the host culture, which underlies so much in Hawai'i, with the addition of customs and values brought by the early settlers from subsistence communities in other rural areas. The unity felt among those who call themselves local also is based on the shared history of plantation life, of social class, and of the prejudice many experienced in the old days of the haole patriarchy.

Some people today, concerned about the Hawaiians' loss of sovereignty, differentiate between Islanders who are local but "settlers," and Islanders who are Native Hawaiian —defined as someone whose ancestors were here before the arrival of Captain Cook. Other words are also subject to interpretation. The word **"kama'āina"** often is applied to anyone who has a Hawai'i driver's license, especially when it comes to getting discounts at tourist attractions. But the word means "child of the land," and **malihini** (newcomers) would be wise to accept that true kama'āina do not consider them to have become kama'āina just because the malihini chose to live in Hawai'i. The most liberal interpretation is "longtime resident." Some believe kama'āina should be used only in reference to Native Hawaiians or to people who were born here.

Some people prefer not to be referred to as "haole." Others (this writer included) see no problem with the word. Someone who grew up here may be called a local haole, in the ever-subtle differentiation between groups in these Islands.

Locals who use "haole" as a negative word do so because the history of Caucasians in Hawai'i tends to make people suspicious of their motivations. From the first sailors who jumped ship to the latest millionaire land speculators, haole have been responsible for foisting many unwelcome changes on the Islands, often with an arrogant attitude that says "our Western way is better."

And even the most well-meaning newcomer may have difficulty adjusting to the cultural stew and the pidgin that defines insider status in Hawai'i.

The Island way

One key to fitting in is to realize that Hawai'i is a place of very strong social capital—those informal bonds and networks that tie people together and create the wealth of human relationships that make a community thrive.

From the Hawaiians' cooperative subsistence economy to the immigrants' dependence on each other for survival in a strange land, the people of Hawai'i have always relied on community. In these cultures, the welfare of the group has first priority. Compare that with the individualistic, self-reliant, mobile culture of the Mainland, and you'll see why some newcomers have trouble making themselves at home in Hawai'i.

One meaning of the word "malihini" is "newcomer;" another is "guest." As a malihini, think of how you would act as a guest in someone's home. Though your host may invite you to make yourself at home, you know that certain basic behaviors are understood. You would probably ask polite questions about your hosts and their family; inquire about any special customs they'd like you to follow in their home; be willing to gracefully accept whatever is served for dinner; and treat their belongings with respect. So it should be for malihini in Hawai'i.

If you plan to stay here, learn to appreciate the differences among cultures. First understand what was here before you, and then contribute your special gifts to the mix. You'll find a key question in discussions of contemporary issues is always, "Is it good for the community?"

As you think about your actions and attitudes as a newcomer in Hawai'i, consider the differences between malihini plants. All plants imported into Hawai'i are considered alien species, but some are also labeled invasive. These plants, coming from a place where survival required that they spread rapidly to smother possible competitors, now pose great danger to the native vegetation of Hawai'i. Native plants evolved in a time and place in which they were able to develop without fear of predators or need for defense mechanisms.

in 'Iao Valley, not far from where I live on Maui, a clump of golden bamboo whose stalks are marked with narrow green stripes grows along the trail. This bamboo is not native to Hawai'i, but it has grown in that spot for years, a decorative plant in a jungle far from its original home. Well established, it stays in its place, content (if plants can be considered content) to flourish in beauty beside the rushing stream.

On the road to Hāna, another species of bamboo grows prolifically. Its thin green stalks spread over acres and acres, climbing hills and filling valleys. Where this bamboo grows, nothing else can survive. It is an invasive species.

As you begin your new life in Hawai'i, resolve to be like the golden bamboo. You are not native to this land; you'll always be, in some sense, an alien species. But like the golden bamboo, you can be an ornament in the garden. Be proud of your own heritage and beauty, while respecting the rights of all the others who grow on these shores.

Island Communities

You could live most of a lifetime on any one of the Hawaiian Islands and never know it completely, and each is different from the others. These profiles give glimpses of the eight major islands. They are arranged from west to east, as the Islands themselves surfaced over eons from beneath the Pacific, and thus begin with the tiny island of Ni'ihau. Ironically, while Ni'ihau was the first island to be visited by Western malihini, it is one of the least likely to be visited by newcomers today.

Ni'ihau

The 72-square-mile island of Ni'ihau, about 18 miles west of Kaua'i, has been privately owned since the 1860s.

An arid island in the rain shadow of Kaua'i, Ni'ihau has three "intermittent" lakes, which fill with water only after a rain. Soft, flexible "makaloa" mats woven from a sedge that grows around these mud flats were highly prized by ancient chiefs on all the islands and perhaps were Ni'ihau's main claim to fame before 1778.

In that year, on his first visit to Hawai'i, Captain James Cook sent two boats and 20 men ashore for supplies. Stranded by high surf for two days, the men were able to acquire a good supply of yams (most of which they lost to the waves). They left behind venereal disease in a Hawaiian population estimated by these first Western visitors at about 500.

Ni'ihau came into private hands after the arrival in 1863 of a family headed by a lively widow named Elizabeth "Eliza" Sinclair. Mrs. Sinclair and her husband, Captain Francis Sinclair, had immigrated from Great Britain to New

Zealand, where the captain and their eldest son disappeared in 1846 while on a sailing voyage. Eliza Sinclair rebuilt her family's fortunes, then led them on a journey to British Columbia aboard a ship called *Bessie*, captained by her son-in-law Thomas Gay. The family intended to settle in Canada, but found conditions there discouraging and headed to Honolulu. Aboard the ship were Eliza Sinclair; Captain Gay, his son by his first marriage, his wife (Eliza's daughter Jean), and their four children; Eliza's daughter Helen Robinson (who had left her husband in New Zealand) and her son, Aubrey; and Eliza's unmarried children Francis, James, and Annie.

Welcomed by the citizens of Honolulu, the family turned down opportunities to buy several large (and eventually very valuable) tracts of land on O'ahu, choosing instead to purchase the island of Ni'ihau. Apparently, unusually rainy weather had made the island green enough to impress Francis and James when they went for an inspection. The family lived there for a while, surviving the death of Captain Gay during a trip to Australia to sell *Bessie* and celebrating the marriage of Annie to Kaua'i rancher and sugar pioneer Valdemar Knudsen.

In 1865, Eliza Sinclair bought the entire ahupua'a of Makaweli, more than 21,000 acres on the south coast of Kaua'i. The family built a spacious home there, where Eliza Sinclair ruled as matriarch of the Sinclair-Robinson-Gay clan while son Francis ran a benevolent patriarchy on Ni'ihau.

Over the years, the family acquired more land, raised sheep, cattle, and horses, and began to grow sugar. Today, Gay & Robinson Inc. is one of the last two sugar plantations in Hawai'i, and the family remains committed to cane cultivation.

Ni'ihau still belongs to members of the family and is off limits to outsiders unless they visit through the family's tour business, which offers beach excursions and hunting for feral sheep and pigs to help keep those populations under control. About 200 residents still live a simple life on the island, with no electricity and school only up to the eighth grade; children may be sent off island to complete their education. The Hawaiian language has remained in everyday use, and Ni'ihau residents were among the Islands' few remaining native speakers when the Hawaiian-immersion preschools were founded to revive the language.

Ni'ihau was the site of an attempted invasion by a single Japanese pilot who landed his disabled plane there after the attack on Pearl Harbor. The pilot managed to persuade one local man of Japanese ancestry to support him, and held a few Ni'ihau residents captive, but a Hawaiian named Benehakaka Kanahele rushed the invader, overcame him despite being hit by three pistol shots, and bashed him against a wall, killing him.

Besides its precious remnant of undiluted Hawaiian language and the kind of self-reliance demonstrated by Ben Kanahele, "The Forbidden Island" is best known today for the exquisite lei made from tiny shells found on its shores and valued into the thousands of dollars.

Kaua'i

Kaua'i is the oldest of the main Hawaiian Islands, formed by a single volcano that rose from the sea six million years ago. More than 60 movies have been filmed on this 533-square-mile island of dramatic cliffs and lush valleys, sometimes called "Hollywood's tropical back lot."

Kaua'i's people have always been known for their independence. When Kamehameha the Great attempted to invade Kaua'i, he was stopped first by stormy weather and then by a plague. Knowing that the conqueror would try again, Kaua'i King Kaumuali'i chose to join the new Hawaiian kingdom through treaty rather than risk his island's well-being. To this day, Kaua'i people are proud that theirs is the only Hawaiian island that was not conquered by the Napoleon of the Pacific.

Kaua'i experienced the Islands' first Western contact when British Captain James Cook arrived in 1778. Like the other Islands, Kaua'i changed greatly after that first visit. Sandalwood forests disappeared as chiefs ordered their people to harvest the fragrant wood for trade. Hawai'i's first commercial sugar plantation was established in 1835, and a mill was built at Kōloa. Sugar planters pursued commercial gain with little thought for preserving native ecosystems.

In the twentieth century, Kaua'i's people rallied to fight inappropriate development and preserve its beauty. They decreed that no building could stand higher than a coconut palm, and established Kōke'e State Park, with more than 4,000 acres of alpine plants, streams, and rare birds.

Like other plantation communities across Hawai'i, Kaua'i saw big changes after World War II, when union organization helped end the custom of company-owned housing. Former plantation camps became subdivisions in Līhu'e, Hanapēpē, Kalāheo, and Puhi, and in the pineapple and ranch lands in and above Kapa'a and Wailua. Tourism development created the "Coconut Coast" on the north shore, and resorts at Po'ipū along the south shore and at Princeville overlooking Hanalei.

One of Hawai'i's two remaining sugar plantations, Gay & Robinson, cultivates land leased from the Robinson family, the island's largest private landowners.

Kaua'i is home to Waimea Canyon (sometimes called the "Grand Canyon of the Pacific"), Mount Wai'ale'ale (one of the wettest spots on earth), and the 20-square-mile Alaka'i Swamp, located at the highest elevation of any swamp on the planet.

More than 50 miles of white sand beaches line Kaua'i's coastline. Hanalei's acres of taro provide more than half the state's poi. On the spectacular Nā Pali Coast, green cliffs rise 2,000 feet high, accessible only by boat or by the ancient Kalalau Trail.

Kaua'i's people have been able to control building on their island to keep it rural and green, and Kaua'i is known for its peacefulness. But even this tight-knit community has no control over forces of nature like Hurricane 'Iniki, which hit in 1992. As neighbors helped each other to recover, they built ties of caring that deepened the island's existing sense of community. Studies document a phenomenon that has become known as the 'Iniki Effect: Kaua'i now leads the state in giving time and money to charities. On Kaua'i, beauty is more than skin deep.

O'ahu

O'ahu was not always the center of things in the Islands. In the century before Western contact, strong chiefly families contended for power and land on Maui and Hawai'i Island.

Captain James Cook sailed by O'ahu in 1778 without noticing the narrow channel that led to a sheltered harbor with a little fishing village called Kou on its shore. Kou sat on the edge of the dusty plain joining the mountain ranges, Ko'olau and Wai'anae, formed by the volcanoes that created O'ahu more than two million years ago.

The Ko'olau Mountains blocked the trade winds from Kou, and the rain fell instead on the windward side of the mountains, where it watered the highly cultivated lands of Kāne'ohe and Kailua.

Not until about 1793 did a Western ship discover the harbor that would give Kou a new name, Honolulu, meaning "protected bay." It soon became a resting place for ships on transpacific voyages.

In 1795, Hawai'i Island Chief Kamehameha defeated the O'ahu army at Nu'uanu Pali. Kamehameha lived for a time near the harbor to keep tabs on its growing commercial activity but eventually returned to his home island, where he ended his days in 1819.

The next year, missionaries arrived from New England. They fought for Hawaiian souls against whalers and ancient tradition in a little town where drunken sailors partied and livestock ran wild.

Honolulu gradually settled down, and in the 1840s became the capital of the kingdom. King Kalākaua built the elegant 'Iolani Palace. The agents, or "factors," who handled business and politics for sugar planters headquartered here, growing into the big businesses that eventually controlled much of life in Hawai'i.

In the 1870s, James Campbell (an Irish carpenter who landed in 1850 on Maui, where he founded the Pioneer Mill plantation) bought a large chunk of arid land west of Pearl Harbor. At the time, this land seemed highly unproductive, but Campbell was a visionary. He drilled the first of Oʻahu's now-famous artesian wells and made agriculture possible. Watered by these deep wells and by irrigation ditches and tunnels bringing water from the windward side, plantations of sugar and pineapple flourished on the dry central plain.

Sugar brought prosperity but also a desire for favorable business conditions among plantation owners. Businessmen led the the 1893 coup that toppled the monarchy and eventually resulted in annexation by the United States.

In little more than a century, the outside world had transformed Oʻahu, and the changes were just beginning. In the 1920s, the Ala Wai Canal drained the wetlands of Waikīkī, a favorite retreat first for Oʻahu ruling chiefs and later for the new haole elite. Gracious hotels, the Moana and the Royal Hawaiian, drew well-heeled tourists.

The attack on Pearl Harbor on December 7, 1941, brought thousands of servicemen to Oʻahu. They returned home to spread the image of the Islands as a symbol of all that is tropical and romantic.

Today, Waikīkī is crowded with visitors, and downtown Honolulu with its glass and steel towers is the sophisticated commercial center of the Pacific. The capital island of the chain includes a busy city, rural towns, and remote wild areas inaccessible by road. Nearly three-quarters of the state's population, or 881,000 people, live on Oʻahu's 608 square miles. Honolulu is home to half the island's population, a collection of people from many cultures. Those who prefer a less-urban hometown often settle in Kailua or Kāneʻohe on the windward side, but many must make the commute into town for work.

In the late 1980s, the Estate of James Campbell began development of Kapolei, Oʻahu's "Second City," on the land west of Pearl Harbor where a century earlier Campbell had drilled that first life-giving well. By 2025, Kapolei is expected to almost equal the 2005 population of Honolulu. Residential development there has surged ahead of job creation, so Kapolei is still something of a bedroom community.

The harbor that brought the city of Honolulu into being remains vital not only to the city's existence but to the entire state. Almost everything imported into Hawai'i (which includes some 80 percent of the state's consumer goods) comes through the harbor. About 3,500 ships arrive in a year, hauling anything from groceries to automobiles to building materials. More than 53 piers and berths are scattered between Sand Island and Kaka'ako. Shipping traffic in and out of the harbor goes on 24 hours a day, all overseen from Aloha Tower.

Back in the days before jet air travel, the harbor and its doings were familiar facets of Honolulu life. Boat Day, when passenger ships arrived, attracted all kinds of people, from lei-sellers to kids diving for coins in the water. Less colorful and more taken for granted these days, the harbor still is essential to the shipping of goods in and out of the Islands. With little warehouse space available in the area, it's a "just-in-time" operation, and Hawai'i routinely gets by with a week's supply of gas and oil and a few days' worth of food on market shelves.

Just inland of the harbor, in the Honolulu Capital Cultural District, civic buildings, museums, historic sites, and galleries cluster within a few square miles, offering windows to the past at 'Iolani Palace, the original missionary houses, and the great Bishop Museum.

More recent history is remembered at Pearl Harbor, where the Arizona Memorial was built over the sunken battleship entombing more than 1,000 crew members who died on December 7, 1941. Nearby is the USS Missouri, where the war ended with the formal Japanese surrender on September 2, 1945.

Away from city streets, lush greenery still covers the mountains and valleys of O'ahu. A beautiful island of spectacular cliffs and breathtaking views, its volcanic origins are visible in the tuff cones of Punchbowl, Diamond Head, and Koko Head, and the great ocean-filled crater of Kāne'ohe Bay.

Moloka'i

Moloka'i is doing its best not to turn out like its big-sister island, Maui. Sometimes called the "most Hawaiian island," with 62 percent of the population identifying itself as Hawaiian or Pacific Islander, Moloka'i is a place where you feel yourself slow down as you leave the airport. Moloka'i people want to keep it that way.

The fifth largest of the archipelago, Moloka'i totals 260 square miles. The population is about 7,000, and half of those live in or near Kaunakakai, a tiny town without even one stoplight. Moloka'i is famous for its ancient fishponds. Remnants of more than 60 ponds remain along the south shore, a couple of which are being reconstructed and once again used for aquaculture.

Legend says that Laka, goddess of the hula, gave birth to the dance here, an event celebrated each year at the annual Moloka'i Ka Hula Piko Festival in May.

One part of Moloka'i, the Hansen's disease colony at Kalaupapa on the Makanalua Peninsula, still houses a few folks who suffered from the disease commonly known as leprosy. This illness, thought to have come from China, arrived in Hawai'i in the 1840s. In 1866, the kingdom began to exile its victims to this isolated peninsula on the north coast of the island. Primitive and sometimes brutal conditions there began to improve with the arrival in 1873 of Father Damien de Veuster, who ministered to the people's needs until his own death from the disease in 1889. Heartbreaking stories are told of families torn apart by the exile to Kalaupapa of people stricken with leprosy. A cure was found in the 1940s, and those who still live in what is now a National Historic Park choose to stay because for them it has become home.

Moloka'i life over the past century has in many ways been dominated by the Moloka'i Ranch, established in 1897. Ranching (and the cherished **paniolo,** or cowboy, tradition) received a major blow in the 1980s, when more than 9,000 cattle were slaughtered in an attempt to eradicate bovine tuberculosis on the island. The ranch, covering about 53,000 acres, for years leased land for pineapple cultivation. Since that industry shut down in 1989, things have been tough on Moloka'i, with the highest unemployment rate in the state. Now called Moloka'i Properties Ltd., the ranch was bought by a New Zealand–based corporation in the 1980s.

Moloka'i people have resisted development for decades, their behavior sometimes seeming to contradict Moloka'i's nickname, "The Friendly Island."

Proud of their rural lifestyle, of their connection to the traditional ways of providing for the family by hunting, fishing, and growing food, Moloka'i people make it a point to stop and talk story in the grocery store or check whether a neighbor needs something before making a trip into town.

Many newcomers are met with suspicion by islanders who fiercely fight outside influence and development, demanding that newcomers respect local ways and being outright confrontational when they don't. In the 1970s, Moloka'i residents fought the ranch to protest restrictive land-use policies and demand access to hunting and fishing grounds. In the process, they helped give birth to the Hawaiian rights movement that eventually reclaimed the island of Kaho'olawe.

More recently, protesters stopped cruise ships from docking at Kaunakakai, making it clear that the little town would not welcome a flood of gawking tourists. Moloka'i people picketed a land auction by software millionaire John McAfee, and then went into combat mode to fight off the ranch's plans to develop La'au Point—demonstrating yet again that Moloka'i intends to fight for self-determination and to keep the laid-back Hawaiian lifestyle its people cherish.

Lāna'i

Little Lāna'i, at 140 square miles, is sixth in size of the Islands. In legend, it was cleared of man-eating spirits by Kaululā'au, son of the chief of Maui, who had been banished to the lonely island after uprooting his father's breadfruit plantings. The spiritual cleanup apparently made Lāna'i suitable for human habitation, for archaeological studies find remains of villages from ancient times.

Chief Kalaniopu'u of Hawai'i Island ravaged Lāna'i in the 1770s. And it was briefly a penal colony for adulterous women during the time of Kamehameha III. Male lawbreakers had been sent to Kaho'olawe, where they were so hungry they decided to swim across the channel to Maui to steal canoes and food. From there, the men who were being punished for adultery paddled to Lāna'i to pick up their women friends and ran away with them to the mountains of Maui.

A small island, Lāna'i relied for water on a single low mountain, Lāna'ihale, to capture moisture from passing clouds. But the usual villains—goats and sheep introduced by Western sailors—chewed the native forest to the ground, destroying most of the island's only watershed.

Lāna'i was the target of grand plans by Walter Murray Gibson, one of the more colorful characters to appear in Hawai'i in the mid-nineteenth century. Gibson worked with the fledgling Mormon population of the kingdom to create a Hawaiian "City of Joseph" in the 1850s. On Lāna'i, the Hawaiian Mormons worked the harsh, dry land to finance Gibson's plan to buy the entire Pālāwai Basin, but were disillusioned when they discovered that the purchase had been registered in Gibson's name. Gibson was excommunicated, and the Mormon community moved to Lā'ie on O'ahu, where they established a successful community (and where the Church of Jesus Christ of Latter-day Saints runs the Hawai'i campus of Brigham Young University).

An early Chinese immigrant living on Lāna'i is said to have been the first man in the kingdom to boil sugar, a crop the Hawaiians grew but did not process. Later attempts to raise the crop commercially on this arid island failed. For a time, the island was used for ranching, and in the 1920s ranch manager George Munro rounded up the destructive wild livestock and replanted the land, most notably with Cook Island pines, which are Lāna'i's trademark tree today.

The island's agricultural fame was born in the twentieth century, when James Dole bought the entire island for $1.1 million and planted 20,000 acres in pineapple.

As the twentieth century drew to a close, pineapple on Lāna'i fell victim to international commerce. Faced with the competition of imported pineapple, Castle & Cook and Dole Foods Company shut down the plantation in 1985 and converted the island to a luxurious vacation destination, with two hotels and two golf courses. Field hands came in out of the sun for training in top-level resort service. Today, most of the population of about 3,200 work either at the English-country-retreat-style Lodge at Kō'ele in the island's highlands or at the lush Mediterranean-style Mānele Bay Hotel on the shore. There's not a lot of choice; Castle & Cooke (itself privately owned by David H. Murdock) owns 98 percent of the island.

The few people who don't work directly for the resort run the tiny town of Lāna'i City, originally established as a plantation town and now home to a few stores and cafés, the small Lāna'i Hotel built by James Dole, the community's schools, a little hospital, and other public facilities. The island also has a population of wealthy transplants who have purchased the residential units Murdock developed.

In 2007, Castle & Cooke announced plans to set up a solar farm at Pālāwai that would provide about a third of the island's energy requirements and to begin studies on growing biofuel crops and producing wind power. If it works out, the wind energy will be pumped via underwater cable to power-hungry O'ahu.

Folks who choose to live on Lāna'i have to be ready for the simple life, with little in the way of entertainment and modern conveniences. Many residents travel to Maui on the ferry to do their shopping, arriving at the dock in Lahaina for the afternoon return trip laden with bags, boxes, and coolers.

Though there is a small airport on the island, the daily ferry offers a wonderful way to visit for those who want to get a taste of the island but can't afford the luxury prices of the Lāna'i resorts. Ferry passengers often see spinner dolphins dancing in the waves as they near Lāna'i, and humpbacks breach in the channel during the winter whale season. The ferry docks at Mānele Harbor, a short walk away from Hulopo'e Beach, where pods of dolphins can be viewed (from a respectful distance) resting in the clear waters of the bay.

Kaho'olawe

Curled like a fetus near the bosom of Mother Maui, Kaho'olawe holds a special place in Hawaiian hearts.

It was here that Hawaiian activists of the 1970s found a focus for their efforts to reclaim their cultural identity and its relationship to the land.

By that time, the island was a devastated wreck, ravaged by the teeth of grazing animals and shattered by military bombs. But the island's almost-forgotten history extended back to the earliest days of Polynesian migration. Before Western contact, fishing villages lined its shores, and it was a navigational center for voyaging, the site of an adze quarry, an agricultural center, and a place for religious and cultural ceremonies. The island has also been called Kanaloa and is dedicated to this god of the ocean.

Hawaiian settlement began the process of denuding the island of trees, but the real destruction came with the introduction of goats, a gift in the late 1700s, probably from Captain George Vancouver to Maui Chief Kahekili, who controlled Kaho'olawe. The creatures multiplied and ate their way through the native vegetation, beginning the degradation that would continue for almost 200 years.

The island served as a penal colony in the 1830s and 1840s, then was leased to a series of ranchers, who introduced yet another destructive animal, the sheep. The most successful of the ranchers was Angus MacPhee, who set out in 1918 to clear the island of goats and sheep and to establish water storage. With the backing of his partner, Maui landowner Harry Baldwin, MacPhee fought recurring drought and was able to maintain herds of cattle and horses.

As World War II loomed, the partners leased part of the island to the U.S. military. After the attack on Pearl Harbor, the Navy took the whole island and used it as a bombing range in preparation for battles in the Pacific. When the war was over, the military kept the island and continued to use it as a bombing target. The remaining goats ran rampant, eventually reaching a population of some 50,000.

By the time young Hawaiians formed the Protect Kaho'olawe 'Ohana in the 1970s, Kaho'olawe's surface had eroded down to hardpan across much of the island. Its red soil ran like blood into the blue ocean, draining life from the island and smothering the rich reefs that surrounded it.

Years of struggle and legal action resulted in a requirement that the U.S. Navy conduct an environmental impact statement and inventory and protect the historic sites on the island. Eventually, some 3,000 archaeological sites were documented, and Kaho'olawe was listed on the National Register of Historic Places. President George Bush Sr. ordered a stop to the bombing, and Hawai'i Senator Daniel K. Inouye led the effort to get Congress to end military use of the island and to authorize $400 million for ordnance removal.

In 1994, the U.S. Navy conveyed ownership of Kaho'olawe to the State of Hawai'i, and the Kaho'olawe Island Reserve Commission was established to manage the island. Between 1997 and 2003 (when the money ran out), 74 percent of the island surface had been cleared, 9 percent of the surface to a depth of 4 feet.

Kaho'olawe remains a focal point of Hawaiian cultural activity. The commission is re-vegetating portions of the island, replacing alien plants with native species, and has installed a rainwater catchment system to provide irrigation. Access to the island and the surrounding waters is restricted, because the unexploded ordnance left by decades of military bombing still pose a danger. The commission also maintains a respectful emphasis on the island's importance to Hawaiian culture and spirituality, integrating cultural practices into all its work there.

Maui

More than a century ago, Hawaiians coined the motto "Maui nō ka 'oi"—Maui is the best. Today, major travel magazines annually name Maui as the world's best island.

Maui is a magical place, like the demigod Māui for whom it is named. A superbeing capable of powerful feats, Māui-of-a-Thousand-Tricks is famous throughout Polynesia, an endearing character whose name symbolizes adventure and creativity.

Like the others in the chain, this island began as magma welling up from the "hot spot" under the Pacific tectonic plate. The volcanoes of West Maui and Haleakalā merged, then joined Moloka'i, Lāna'i, and Kaho'olawe to form Maui Nui, or Great Maui. Long since separated by the sea, the islands are still politically connected as Maui County. Second in size of the islands, Maui is 728 square miles.

Lahaina, the political capital of the kingdom until the mid-1840s, was a favorite of the chiefs and of the whalers who wintered in the Islands.

The whaling industry came to Hawai'i in 1820, when ships seeking sperm whales in the Northern Pacific found Hawai'i a convenient place for rest and recuperation. Lahaina offered open anchorage and fresh produce. During the heyday of whaling, 1840 to 1860, more than 400 ships visited Lahaina's port in some years, and the town boomed with grog shops and sailors in pursuit of female company.

The hard-living whalers' taste for partying resulted in frequent conflict with the missionaries, who were busily converting the natives and setting up schools like Lahaina-luna, the first secondary school west of the Rockies.

When whaling declined, agriculture took its place, and sugar became king. By the early 1900s, Maui life centered around sugar, pineapple, and cattle ranching.

World War II brought thousands of American warriors to rest and train in Maui's jungles and beaches and sent many of its young men to fight abroad.

After the war, with bright young people leaving and the sugar industry struggling against competition, the Maui economy stagnated. County leaders encouraged the establishment of the visitor industry, beginning with the building of Kā'anapali, the world's first master-planned destination resort. Next, water piped in from Central Maui made it possible to develop the sunny south coast.

Maui was on its way to becoming world-famous.

Today, parts of the old Maui still exist amid the hustle and bustle of a community that often suffers from growing pains, with crowded roads, water and housing shortages, and a general nostalgia for the way things used to be. Still, Maui is gorgeous, dotted with little towns on an island of micro climates; if you don't like the weather where you are, a short drive will take you to someplace entirely different.

The major population areas are in Central Maui, the broad plain that connects Haleakalā and the West Maui Mountains. Wailuku, the county seat, blends into Kahului, created when plantations wanting to get out of the housing business made fee-simple homes available around the old Port Town of the harbor. Kahului became the commercial center of the island, with major shopping centers and big-box stores. Across the isthmus, the dry and sunny coastal community of Kīhei has evolved from a kiawe forest just a few decades ago to one of the state's fastest-growing communities, with luxury hotels down the coast in Wailea.

The western slopes of Haleakalā are known as Upcountry. The surrounding green pastures and stunning views make Upcountry towns highly desirable residential communities, and the Kula area is also still known for the rich farming soil that made its Irish potatoes a favorite with the miners of the California Gold Rush. Down the mountain, the old plantation town of Pā'ia once was home to 10,000, many of them sugar workers. Now it's a funky little tourist town. Keep going east, and you'll eventually end up in Hāna, the tiny town at the end of the dramatically beautiful jungle-bordered Hāna Highway.

West Maui is almost an island on its own. The Kingdom of Hawai'i's first capital and a favorite playground of nineteenth-century whalers, Lahaina was a sugar town for years but now makes its living on tourism. Like its neighbors to the west, from Kā'anapali to Kapalua, this sunny seaside community lives with the knowledge that the Pali Highway, its lifeline to essential services in Central Maui, can be cut at any time by traffic accidents, rock-fall, or brushfire.

Hawai'i

Hawai'i Island is the youngest of the chain, still being born as lava pours from the Earth to build new land. It earns its nickname, the Big Island, by being large enough at 4,028 square miles to hold all seven of the other main islands with room to spare. Its weather is more diverse than any other comparably sized piece of land in the world, ranging from Puna's tropical rain forests to Kohala's desert to the chilly peaks of Mauna Kea and Mauna Loa.

In Hilo, on the east side, as much as 165 inches of rain each year creates lush greenery. The sunny Kona coast attracts tourists with warm, dry days and clear waters, great for snorkeling, scuba diving, and deep-sea fishing. Waimea's green pastures lie above rich resorts planted amid old lava flows edged with white sand beaches. In the more remote districts like Ka'u and Puna, life is simple and rural, with many residents living self-reliant lifestyles off the grid.

None of the five volcanoes that built this island is considered truly extinct, but only two have been active in recent decades. Mauna Loa last erupted in 1984. Kīlauea began a long-lasting eruption in 1983 from a vent known as Pu'u 'Ō'ō, wiping out dozens of structures and some famous landmarks while adding many acres of land along the Puna coastline.

Hawaiian legend says this island is headquarters of the fire goddess Pele, who left her original home on a perhaps mythical island to the southwest and traveled first to the northwest islands of Hawai'i. Moving south, Pele searched for a home at each island, but only when she reached Hawai'i Island was she successful in digging deep with her magic stick without striking water, an element incompatible with her fiery nature. Pele now lives in Halema'uma'u, the giant crater at Hawa'i Volcanoes National Park.

The park offers an awe-inducing glimpse into the planet's geological processes. Steam drifts from vents in solidified lava where native trees and ferns have somehow gained a foothold. The air smells of sulfur, and the landscape is alternately bleak (where recent eruptions have covered the land) and lush (where ancient forests have escaped the flowing lava and new forests have taken root). The little village of Volcano right outside the park is home to a small community of scientists and artists.

Hawai'i is the home island of Kamehameha the Great, who was born in North Kohala and reared in Waipi'o Valley. Hawai'i's first king spent much time on the Kona coast, where he died in 1819.

In 1793, British Captain George Vancouver brought Kamehameha a gift of the Islands' first cattle. The king put a kapu on them, forbidding anyone to touch the beasts so they could multiply. That they did, and soon the countryside swarmed with wild cattle. In 1809, young American sailor John Parker jumped ship and went to work for the king. A few years later, Kamehameha allowed Parker to begin shooting the mavericks. Parker's salt beef, along with hides and tallow, became important export items. Parker married a chief's daughter named Kipikane and in 1847 founded the Parker Ranch in Waimea. The 150,000-acre spread is one of the country's largest ranches. Broadway actor Richard

Smart, the last heir to the ranch, established a foundation whose revenues are used for charitable purposes in Waimea.

While ranching became a way of life in Waimea, sugar took root around Hilo and Hamakua. After the industry shut down in the 1990s, diversified agriculture began to fill empty fields with bananas, ginger, and other plants that love the moisture of the island's east side. Big Island farms also grow many kinds of exotic tropical fruits, macadamia nuts, flowers, and trees for wood pulp.

East Hawai'i's main town and the county seat, peaceful Hilo is a serene place of quaint architecture and green parks, with shops featuring exquisite arts and crafts, an open-air fish market, and a flower-filled farmers market. It's a beautiful little city, with Mauna Kea and Mauna Loa looming behind it. Mauna Kea's peaks are often topped with snow in the winter months.

The town is so low-key it's hard to believe that Hilo is the state's second-largest community. Each year it hosts the Merrie Monarch Festival, the world championship of hula. Hilo also is home to the University of Hawai'i at Hilo, the only university-level branch of the state system outside O'ahu. UH-Hilo recently opened the 'Imiloa Astronomy Center on nine acres in the Science and Technology Park above the campus, where multimedia displays in Hawaiian and English tell stories of the rich traditions of Hawaiian culture and of Mauna Kea, home to the world's largest astronomical observatory, with telescopes operated by astronomers from eleven countries.

Hilo also has the dubious distinction of having suffered the most from tsunamis hitting the Islands in recent decades. The 1946 tsunami arrived on April 1, leading some to believe that warnings were an April Fool's joke and resulting in 179 deaths. Another deadly wave hit in 1960, killing 61 people. Hilo now maintains open space along the shoreline, where the waves wiped out whole chunks of the town.

On the west side of the island, Kona's sunny mountain-sides of rich volcanic soil have produced the famous hand-picked Kona coffee for more than 150 years. In Kona, history seems close, with ancient fishponds, a 700-year-old heiau, a royal summer palace, and Hawai'i's oldest surviving Christian church. Still, the little town of Kailua-Kona buzzes with activity. It's a tourist center for fun, shopping, and deep-sea fishing boats. Just mauka, tiny communities along the winding two-lane highway offer art galleries and beautiful bed-and-breakfast getaways. The area has boomed in recent years, becoming the commercial and tourist center of West Hawai'i and filling with new residents whose presence has led to rapid development and increasing traffic congestion.

Mixed Plate

Newcomers have a lot to learn as they fit into Island life; the ingredients of this unique lifestyle are a mix of the host Hawaiian culture with customs brought by people from around the world. The following pages will give you practical suggestions for learning to live in Hawai'i and help you understand the origins of some of the language and customs you'll encounter on a daily basis.

A few hints on pronouncing Hawaiian words

In a preliterate, oral culture, Hawaiians learned by listening, and newcomers would be well advised to do the same. Listen to Hawaiian music and to the Hawaiian Word of the Day on Hawai'i Public Radio. The only Hawaiian language news broadcast in the state, Ke Aolama, is on KIPO 89.3 every morning around 8:30. Pay attention to how local newscasters and performers pronounce Hawaiian words. Learn to separate words into syllables, and pronounce each one separately, then blend together. Here are some helpful hints.

❖ Pronounce vowels as if they were Spanish, Latin, or Italian. Like this:

> *A* as in father
> *E* as in bait
> *I* as in meet
> *O* as in hope
> *U* as in toot

❖ Every word has at least one vowel, and every word ends with a vowel.

❖ There are no consonant clusters—vowels always separate consonants.

❖ General rules for "w": If it begins the word or follows *u* or *o*, it sounds like "w"—Waikīkī, Olowalu. If it follows *i* or *e*, it sounds like a soft "v"—Ewa, Haleiwa. If it follows *a*, use your ears to learn the common pronunciation. It could be "w" but is usually "v," as in Kaho'olawe or Waiawa. One of the few words with a "w-after-a" sound: Wahiawā.

❖ The 'okina, or glottal stop, is a consonant, and sounds something like the break between the two "ohs" in "oh-oh." The 'okina may begin a word or be inserted between vowels.

❖ The kahakō, or macron, is a short horizontal line above a vowel to indicate that it is stressed, or longer than other vowels. The 'okina and kahakō can change the meanings of words, so they should be used if possible. You need special fonts on your computer to generate them, and many language experts suggest that if you don't have the fonts you should not try to get by with just a substitute 'okina using existing keys, either the apostrophe or the key with the ~. It's not correct to use just the 'okina without the kahakō. You can buy Hawaiian fonts from Guava Graphics (www.guavagraphicshawaii.com) or download a few for free from www.olelo.hawaii/edu.

❖ If you are going to use 'okina and kahakō, look them up and use them correctly. Don't casually scatter 'okina where you think they belong! Standard references are *Hawaiian Dictionary* (Pukui and Elbert) and *Place Names of Hawai'i* (Pukui, Elbert, and Mookini).

❖ The adjective follows the noun in Hawaiian. For example, "pretty flower" is "pua nani"—literally "flower pretty."

❖ Plurals are indicated by "na," not by an "s" on the end of the word. Say "na pua," not "puas."

Why do all those Hawaiian words start with "K"?

The words for "the," singular, are "ke" and "ka." Many Hawaiian names are actually phrases or compound words: Kealakekua (the pathway [of] the god); Kalaniana'ole (the royal chief without measure); Kaho'olawe (the carrying away, as by currents).

Some common phrases

Pehea 'oe? (How are you?)
Maika'i no. (I'm well.)
Aloha kakahiaka. (Good morning.)
Mahalo nui loa. (Thank you very much.)
He mea iki. (You're welcome—literally, "a small thing.")
A hui hou (Good-by; 'til we meet again.)

Pidgin

Like all languages, Hawai'i pidgin changes. Beginning with the original patchwork of tongues that allowed immigrants from different lands to communicate and evolving into the first language of many modern Islanders, pidgin doesn't sound now the way it sounded in the 1800s. In fact, modern speakers might have a hard time following a conversation between plantation workers of a century ago. Pidgin can sound different on different islands. And when Islanders speak standard English, they often have a distinctive regional accent that draws on the rich history of language in Hawai'i.

Attitudes toward pidgin have changed from the days when it was viewed as broken English. Modern linguists tell us that pidgin is a language, just as English is a language, and there is room for the two to coexist peacefully. Today, pidgin is used in public service announcements, commercials, and serious literature, including poetry.

If you have children, chances are they will pick up pidgin easily from their playmates. If you intend to live here, that's probably a very good thing, because pidgin is one of the ties that keeps the local community cohesive. Don't worry; as long as they already speak standard English and know how to use it, they will be able to switch according to the situation they are in, and speaking pidgin will be a social advantage.

On the other hand, adults who move here should stick to their own manner of speaking. As years go by, you will find your speech sprinkled with phrases and intonations acquired through familiarity with the local patois, but trying to sound local when it doesn't come naturally just won't work. If you did not grow up here, do not try to speak pidgin. Period.

But you do need to understand pidgin, because you will hear it often and may need to communicate with people for whom this is a primary language. Simply hearing pidgin over a period of time will help, but you can also learn some words and phrases from the *Pidgin to Da Max* books.

 Locals Know: Did you just get your youngest child into high school, only to discover that there's another one on the way? This surprise baby is your "ratoon crop," a term borrowed from Hawai'i agriculture. Both sugar and pineapple produce a bonus harvest when the ratoon crop sprouts from a field that already has been harvested, and Islanders have borrowed the term for those unexpected late babies.

"Local style"

These examples of cultural values are of course generalities. Still, it is interesting to see how the various ethnicities brought customs honed by years of living in small rural communities to form a "local" culture that contrasts with the more competitive style of Western civilization. Local-style culture tends to be polite, cooperative, reciprocal, and family oriented. This list is adapted from information found in *People and Cultures of Hawaii: A Psychocultural Profile*, which is listed in the Recommended Reading section at the end of this book.

Hawaiian

- ❖ 'Ohana—Strong family ties and relationships
- ❖ Lōkāhi—Unity, social harmony. Confrontations and conflicts avoided
- ❖ Seeking gain for the sake of the group rather than for oneself
- ❖ Indirectness valued—relax and "talk story" rather than asking direct questions
- ❖ Hospitality, sharing

Chinese

- ❖ Extended family system
- ❖ Impolite to deny requests; avoidance of conflict
- ❖ Inner thoughts kept to themselves, especially if negative
- ❖ Extreme concern for interpersonal relationships to preserve order within the family
- ❖ Hard work and money valued for support of family, education, the aged, land ownership

Japanese

- ❖ Oriented to the group rather than the individual
- ❖ Sense of obligation to family and country and reciprocity between individuals (for example, much gift giving)
- ❖ Graceful acceptance of what is
- ❖ Hard work, thrift, planning for the future
- ❖ Control of emotional expression in public

Filipino

- ❖ Loyalty to large extended family; neighborliness if no family around
- ❖ Authoritarian structure—leader-follower, teacher-pupil, boss-subordinate

❖ Avoidance of confrontation in order to maintain social relationships
❖ Obligation to repay favors

Local grinds (also known as food)

Hawaiian

❖ Kālua pig: A complete pig cooked whole in an underground oven known as an imu
❖ Laulau: Individual servings of meat or fish wrapped in green taro leaves and cooked with a pig in the imu
❖ Lomi salmon: Salted salmon mixed with chopped tomatoes and onion—a dish actually invented by whalers
❖ Haupia: Coconut pudding
❖ Kūlolo: Taro pudding
❖ Poi: The Hawaiians' staple food, made by mashing the cooked corms of the taro plant into a smooth paste
❖ 'Ulu: Breadfruit, a starch that grows on a beautiful tree and can be cooked in a number of ways
❖ Limu: Seaweed
❖ Poke: Seafood salad, often very spicy. Eaten as a pūpū—a snack or hors d'oeuvre—preferably with cold beer

Japanese

❖ Bento: A box lunch usually including rice, fish cake, shoyu chicken, teriyaki beef
❖ Kamaboko: Fish cake, usually white with a pink edge, often seen in saimin
❖ Miso: Soup made with soybean flavoring
❖ Mochi: Soft little rice cookies, especially made for the New Year celebration
❖ Musubi: Rice balls, sometimes with ume (pickled plum) inside. The most popular contemporary musubi is made with a slice of SPAM held onto the rice with a sheet of nori.

- Nori: Seaweed
- Sashimi: Raw fish
- Shoyu: Soy sauce
- Sushi: Rice and bits of fish or vegetables wrapped in a sheet of nori or stuffed into a shell made of fried tofu (aburage)
- Tempura: Vegetables or seafood dipped in batter and deep-fried
- Tofu: Soybean curd, used in many local dishes
- Teriyaki: Meat or fish marinated in a shoyu sauce, then grilled or broiled

Portuguese

- Malassadas: Pastry like a doughnut without a hole
- Linguiça: Portuguese sausage—a spicy pork sausage that is a staple of local-style breakfasts
- Portuguese soup: A hearty soup made with kidney beans, vegetables and Portuguese sausage
- Portuguese sweetbread (pao doce, pronounced *pawn dulss*): Round loaf of white bread, which used to be baked in backyard wood-fired ovens

Chinese

- All varieties of Chinese food are eaten in Hawai'i, including some that have become part of "local" cuisine.
- Almond pudding: White gelatin flavored with almond extract
- Char siu: Cooked pork with red coloring
- Crack seed: Preserved fruit—pickled, salted, or dried; a favorite snack
- Dim sum: Dumplings filled with meat, seafood, and vegetables
- Manapua: A popular dim sum with char siu inside

Filipino

- Bagoong: Very strong-flavored fish sauce
- Lumpia: Egg roll

❖ Pork or chicken adobo: A sweet-sour dish made with vinegar, soy sauce, and sugar
❖ Pancit: Filipino chop suey

Korean
❖ Kal bi: Korean short ribs
❖ Kim chee: A hot, strong-smelling mix of cabbage, cucumber, or turnips soaked in chili pepper sauce

Only in Hawai'i

Some foods seem to exist only here, created out of the fusion of cultures and the sharing of food.

❖ Huli huli chicken: "Huli" means "to turn" in Hawaiian. Huli huli chicken is a barbecued chicken turned so that it is done on both sides. The phrase is a trademark of an O'ahu company, so legally should be used only for that company's products.
❖ Loco-moco: Rice topped with a hamburger patty or SPAM and fried egg, covered in gravy
❖ Plate lunch: Two scoops rice; macaroni or potato salad; a bit of lettuce, cabbage, or corn; and a meat item consisting of anything from hamburger steak to teriyaki
❖ Pūpū: A snack or hors d'oeuvre
❖ Shoyu chicken: Chicken cooked in a sauce made with shoyu, sugar, garlic, and other ingredients

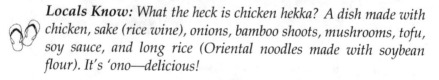

Locals Know: What the heck is chicken hekka? A dish made with chicken, sake (rice wine), onions, bamboo shoots, mushrooms, tofu, soy sauce, and long rice (Oriental noodles made with soybean flour). It's 'ono—delicious!

Hawaiian Style

Hawai'i's characteristic styles of music, dance, dress, and humor express the Islands' beauty and culture, making it unlike any place in the world. These styles often are admired and even adopted outside Hawai'i, but only here does their combined and sustained presence create the ambience of Island life. While they are ever-changing in response to contemporary influence, these styles are rooted in history—in the ancient ways of Hawai'i and in the customs brought by succeeding waves of immigrant groups.

The music

The sweet sounds of Hawai'i's music seem to rise from the heart of the Islands, keeping time with the swaying palms and the rhythm of waves. Its melodies cast a romantic spell that immediately brings to mind pictures of paradise.

Hawai'i's music is loved all over the world. From Sweden to Japan, musicians play songs that tell of a mountain on Maui, a Big Island love affair, or a moonlit night on Kaua'i.

Hula, lei, and the 'ukulele: symbols of Hawai'i

It all began with the chant. In the oral culture of old Hawai'i, the chanter was an important member of society, preserver of history and legend. Though ancient chants, **oli** or **mele,** had little of what Westerners would recognize as melody, they were arranged in complex and changing rhythms, and chanters cultivated distinctive voice styles.

Melody came with the missionaries in 1820. Hawaiians were immediately enthusiastic about this new kind of music. A book of hymns translated into Hawaiian was an instant best-seller. Islanders soon were composing songs in the new style, meshing simple gospel melodies with the beautiful poems and complex rhythms of Hawai'i. Even royalty got into the act. Four noble siblings were especially prolific. Known as the Royal Composers, they were King Kalākaua, Queen Lili'uokalani, Prince Leleiōhoku, and Princess Likelike. Their songs still are loved and sung today. Lili'uokalani composed *Aloha 'Oe,* perhaps the best-known Hawaiian song in the world.

Like the queen, whose *Aloha 'Oe* ends with the line "until we meet again," Hawaiians sometimes sprinkled English words among their lyrics to give them a certain spice. In the early twentieth century, English song writers speakers reversed the trend and began to compose songs with a hint of Hawaiian added.

These "hapa haole" (half foreign) songs first were spread by Hawaiian bands touring the Mainland in the early 1900s. They gained a nationwide audience when "Hawai'i Calls" began broadcasts from the Moana Hotel in 1935, inspiring dreams of paradise in many a Midwesterner. Hapa haole songs are the ones Mainlanders are most likely to have heard and are most likely to remember, for the simple reason that their lyrics are intelligible to those who don't speak Hawaiian. They include oldies like *Little Brown Gal* and lovely tunes such as *Waikīkī, Hanalei Moon,* and *Honolulu City Lights.*

When the hapa haole genre ventured into the wider world, it took along the 'ukulele and the steel guitar. Both instruments became popular outside Hawai'i and remained so even when the touring hapa haole bands disappeared.

The rhythms of the ancient chants had been created by implements made from natural items like stones and gourds. Outsiders introduced stringed instruments such as the braguinha, a small four-stringed guitar brought by Portuguese immigrants in 1879. The Hawaiians named it 'ukulele, which means "jumping flea," perhaps because of the player's rapidly moving fingers.

A favorite of King Kalākaua, the 'ukulele became a fad on the U.S. Mainland in the days of Tin Pan Alley and raccoon coats. The Mainland craze died out, but the 'ukulele never lost its standing in Hawaiian music and today is the specialty of virtuosos like Herb Ohta or the amazing young Jake Shimabukuro.

A Kamehameha Schools student is usually credited with inventing the steel guitar in the 1880s. Joe Kekuku made a steel bar in the school shop and slid it along the strings of a guitar laid across his lap, while plucking notes with his other hand. Musicians like Sol Hoopii etched the sound of Hawaiian steel guitar into national consciousness in Hollywood movies of the 1930s. Players of country-western music adopted the instrument's moody, wailing sound. And when the audiences grew so big that the unamplified steel guitar couldn't be heard, musicians and inventors figured out ways to electrify the instrument, bringing about the most significant change in the history of the guitar.

Two techniques also contribute to the unique sound of Hawaiian music: slack key and falsetto.

Slack key refers to a number of guitar tunings in which some of the strings are loosened, or slackened. The strings are predominantly plucked, rather than strummed, for a lilting, melodic sound. Modern masters include Raymond Kane, Keola Beamer, and Ledward Ka'apana.

Falsetto may have its origins in some of the vocal styles used by ancient chanters, or may have evolved from later influences, perhaps the yodeling of the Hawaiian cowboy, or paniolo. Some female singers use falsetto techniques, such as veteran Auntie Genoa Keawe and young stars Amy Hanaiali'i Gilliom and Raiatea Helm, but it is traditionally associated with male singers like Mahi Beamer, Dennis Pavao, and the Ho'opi'i Brothers.

The music continues to evolve: The 'ukulele may be electrically amplified; Hawaiians are singing "Jawaiian" (a local adaptation of Jamaican reggae); steel drums and congas have been added to the mix. Performers like Keali'i Reichel and Willie K. blend contemporary sounds into the traditional. And a new generation of composers creates lyrics in the reviving Hawaiian language.

In 2005, the Grammy Awards included a Hawaiian music category, won in its first years by collections of slack key melodies by various artists. The Hawaiian Music Hall of Fame celebrated its tenth anniversary that year, and Hawaiian musicians released about 170 new albums.

Hawaiian music now belongs to the world. But its spirit belongs to its birthplace. The lovely words of the Islands' poetic language, sweet tunes sung in falsetto against the lively chords of the 'ukulele, the sinuous tones of a steel guitar, and the intricate notes of slack key—all combine to enchant a listener with the musical essence of Hawai'i.

 Locals Know: If you can't help humming along to your favorite Hawaiian tunes, a Kaua'i program offers an opportunity to actually learn to sing the words. For more than two decades, E Kanikapila Kākou (Let's Play Music) has brought performers and audiences together for informal gatherings attended by kama'āina and newcomers who love to sing Hawaiian music. Those who attend get a song sheet, so they can join in to sing along with well-known Island musicians. The 12-week music festival begins in early February. It's held at the Island School Main Hall, adjacent to Kaua'i Community College in Puhi. There's no charge, but drop a generous donation into the calabash before you sit down to sing your heart out with some of the Islands' best performers.

The dance

The hula maiden, with swaying hips and "lovely hula hands," is a legendary symbol of Hawai'i. But this art form, passed down through generations, is far more than a pretty dance.

The hula of old Hawai'i, now called kahiko (ancient, old), was a ritual of religion and communication. Kahiko is exciting to watch, its performers strong and precise as they move to the beat of the drum and the chanter's call. Dancers wear clothing based on ancient Hawaiian garb—simple cotton tops, skirts, or loincloths printed to look like kapa (or even real kapa), ti leaf skirts, and ferns or vines woven into lei for the neck, head, wrists, and ankles.

In the old days, children were selected in childhood or even before birth for hula training. They spent their formative years separated from the outside world, under the care of a kumu hula, or hula master, and their lives were dedicated to the goddess Laka, patron of the hula. Chants and dance preserved the history of a people's births, deaths, loves, and battles. Hula was danced for religious purposes and also as entertainment, in hope of successful crops or battles, at funerals, or to celebrate human fertility.

The first visitors to Hawai'i didn't understand that the dance held a vital place in the spiritual life of their hosts. Early sailors and traders saw what they wanted to see: semi-nude women with undulating hips.

When the missionaries arrived, they were shocked by dance they considered provocative and "lascivious." They had come to convert these people, and though the New Englanders were willing to accept the Hawaiians' language in order to preach, this dancing had to go. For many years in the nineteenth century, missionary disapproval drove the hula underground.

Hula survived partly because some royalty continued to support it, and partly because dedicated families and individuals in out-of-the-way places quietly continued to pass along their knowledge to succeeding generations.

King David Kalākaua, remembered as the Merrie Monarch for his love of song and dance, sparked a brief cultural renaissance in the 1880s. The hula schools came out of hiding, and dancers performed at his coronation and again at his 50th birthday party.

Kalākaua's fascination with things foreign also helped bring about the style of modern hula called 'auwana (to wander, drift, go astray). Dancers in his time began to include the steps of contemporary popular dances, and they moved to the gliding rhythms of the guitar and 'ukulele rather than the dramatic beat of the pahu (drum) and ipu (gourd). The dress of today's dancers often reflects the elegant European styles of Hawai'i's royal court. 'Auwana is the form of hula most familiar to the outside world.

After Kalākaua died, and his sister Lili'uokalani lost her throne, hula began a long decline into the twentieth century. When Hawaiian music became a fad in the early 1900s, people who never had been to Hawai'i wrote songs and danced what they claimed to be hula on Mainland stages. The sacred dance of Hawai'i was cheapened by a hootchie-koochie image.

Ironically, while Hollywood went crazy over Hawai'i, the culture was suppressed in the Islands, where some Hawaiian families forbade their children to learn to speak Hawaiian or to dance hula.

Still, the image of the lovely hula dancer spread around the world. Military people stationed in the Islands during World War II went home with memories of lilting Hawaiian tunes and a smattering of hula learned from friendly Islanders. And in Island backyards and living rooms, the real culture survived as elders continued to teach their arts to the young.

When the revival of Hawaiian pride began in the 1970s, the dancers were ready. Once more the chant was heard and the flashing movements of kahiko were seen in public.

Now the hula is in full flower. Young and old again dedicate themselves to the hula and to the lifestyle that surrounds it. They grow or gather lei materials, make their own costumes and ornaments, and learn the Hawaiian language of songs and chants.

Today, most hula shows include at least a few dances in the kahiko style, along with the graceful swaying of the 'auwana. And families that have preserved the tradition for generations are stepping out in new directions, maintaining the discipline of their ancestors while innovating with chants and dances for our time.

In recent years, hula and Hawaiian music have spread around the globe. Leading kumu hula grew concerned that many students and even some teachers of the thousands of hālau worldwide had never been to Hawai'i. To remedy this, they organized the World Conference on Hula, held in 2001 in Hilo and in 2005 on Maui. The next will probably be held in 2009 on O'ahu. Hundreds of dancers attend these gatherings, to experience the physical place that is hula's home, to learn more about the arts that surround the dance, and to accept the kuleana, or responsibility, that is at the heart of the dance: the preservation of Hawai'i's culture.

 Locals Know: We are living in a golden age of Hawaiian music and dance, and it doesn't get any better than the performances by today's stars at the Maui Arts & Cultural Center. OK, I know this is blatantly Maui centric, but this facility is in a class of its own. The MACC's 1,200-seat Castle Theater in Kahului provides an elegant setting and excellent acoustics for performers who feel right at home in front of an audience that is, often quite literally, family. Planning a Maui visit? Check the MACC's site at www.mauiarts.org to see if you can make it to one of these incredible events. Another great venue: Honolulu's historic 1,400-seat Hawai'i Theatre, a 1922 building beautifully renovated in the 1990s. And pay attention to entertainment calendars in your own community, because, even if the venues aren't as fancy as these two, the performers are just as great. After all, this is the world center of this type of music and dance; no place on the planet can match what we have right here. Take advantage of it!

The lei

The lei is one of Hawai'i's most recognizable symbols. Its origins are lost in time; no one knows exactly when the Polynesians began to use garlands woven from fresh leaves and flowers as ornaments of worship, but the original settlers brought the lei with them to Hawai'i. Here, the custom evolved to include a greater and richer variety of lei than any other Polynesian island group, and people began to use the lei not just for worship or as a gift to the chief, but as a way to decorate themselves or to express aloha. In Hawai'i today, a lei is appropriate to wear or give for any special occasion, symbolizing love, respect, and pride, or even sympathy at the loss of a loved one.

A lei is not necessarily made of flowers. Other common materials are seeds, shells, leaves, or feathers. Two wonderful books by Marie A. McDonald (*Ka Lei: The Leis of Hawai'i* and *Na Lei Makamae: The Treasured Lei*, written with Paul Weissich) illustrate the ingenuity with which lei makers have used many materials.

Ancient chiefs wore the lei niho palaoa, a hook-shaped pendant carved from a whale's tooth and attached to coils of finely braided human hair. These ornaments are now museum pieces, though the hook-shaped pendant still appears in modern jewelry. The feather lei also indicated chiefly status; the scarcity of materials and the craft required to work with them lent feather lei great value. Kukui nut lei carry the notion of enlightenment, because the oily nut provided the Hawaiians' source of night lighting. Maile, a fragrant green vine growing high in the mountains, is twisted to form long strands that are worn over the shoulders and often are stretched across the front door at a grand opening or house blessing. The maile lei has a particularly celebratory quality, and its scent is wonderful and long lasting.

The most familiar style of lei today is the "kui" lei, a single strand of flowers strung through the center. Now often made with nonnative flowers such as plumerias or orchids, the kui lei in ancient times was used to string the cherished golden 'ilima and the orange blossoms of the kou tree.

More complex "haku" lei are made with great artistry by attaching flowers, foliage, and dried plant material to a backing, sometimes by winding with a piece of cordage, sometimes by braiding. These lei have become even more beautiful as native plant species are available for home gardens, allowing talented lei makers to produce intricate designs with the delicate beauty of native materials.

If you're going to a graduation ceremony, be sure to arrive at commencement with at least one lei for your graduate. Buried beneath a fragrant mound of lei, graduates in Hawai'i peer through piles of flowers, maile, and lei made with ribbon or yarn, coins, candy, or origami-folded currency. The image is so typical that even lei-bedecked politicians on election night are described as looking like graduates. Many a family spends graduation morning scouring the trees, shrubs, and vines around their neighborhood for blossoms to congratulate not only their own graduate, but their child's friends as well.

At one time, it was common for ladies to wear a lei for any dressy occasion, and following a custom established in the late 1920s everyone wore lei on May Day. These days, lei are less common at social gatherings, and many people simply forget to wear a lei when May 1 comes around. Though the fragrance, color, and beauty of the lei are still cherished, somehow there seem to be fewer of them in these hectic days. Go ahead, be old fashioned—plant a plumeria tree or some fragrant tuberose or stephanotis, all easy to string and lovely to wear, and wear a lei out to dinner or a party. If you feel really ambitious, grow native plants and learn to make spectacular haku-style lei, or even the beautiful feather lei, and help keep this tradition alive.

Some lei etiquette: Wear a lei draped across your shoulders, not dangling from your neck like a necklace. A lei is usually given with a kiss; nothing too dramatic, just a quick peck will do. And don't wear a lei you bought or made for someone else—it would be like wearing a shirt before giving it as a gift. But it's OK to share the aloha by passing along a lei that was given to you, even if you have worn it.

Aloha attire

When the first Christian missionaries arrived in 1820, they unwittingly started a fashion revolution. The female chiefs were immediately enamored of the American women's dresses.

The ali'i wahine put the missionary ladies to work stitching up dresses with fabric acquired from sandalwood traders. The seamstresses adapted their own pattern to a loose gown for the Hawaiians' generous figures, creating a new design that would be known as a holokū. It was the beginning of the tradition of clothing designed for Hawai'i, a hand-stitched precursor to the long-running fashion trend and multimillion-dollar industry we call aloha wear.

Before Western contact, Hawaiians wore simple

garments of kapa, a papery fabric made from mulberry bark. Their kapa was some of the finest in the Pacific. Kapa-making was women's work; they pounded the bark to a fine, soft texture, dyed it in a rainbow of colors with berries, leaves, or seeds, and decorated it by painting and block printing. Even high-ranking ladies participated in this artistic endeavor.

But a length of kapa wrapped around the waist or draped over the shoulders left a lot of skin exposed. Once the missionaries landed, they encouraged the Hawaiians to dress haole style, finding it appalling that the islanders often casually dispensed with even what little they wore.

The first design, the holokū, consisted of yards of fabric attached to a yoke, with a high neck and long sleeves. Underneath, women wore a shorter, simpler slip, called a mu'umu'u (cut off, shortened). The mu'umu'u also was worn for sleeping, or for swimming in this newly modest Christian kingdom.

The men, meanwhile, had traded with visiting sailors for the loose shirts, or "frocks," the sailors wore untucked outside their trousers. Some of the shirts were made of a heavy cotton cloth with a blue-and-white plaid pattern that came to be associated with plantation life and took its name —palaka—from the Hawaiian pronunciation of frock.

It was not until the 1930s that the shirts began to be made of more colorful stuff, Japanese kimono prints or simple Asian two-color designs. A shirtmaker named Ellery Chun trademarked the term "aloha shirt" in 1936, and had artists design fabrics. Others sewed shirts of the "bark cloth" tropical prints originally made for draperies and upholstery.

Some shirtmakers tried rayon, but its quality was poor until the 1940s. Postwar Hawai'i still swarmed with servicemen when the new, high-quality rayon became popular, and many of them took home a shirt or two. The war had curtailed shipping, encouraging local manufacture and design. The "aloha wear" industry was under way.

Hawaiian prints gained popularity as manufacturers commissioned artists to create colorful tropical fabrics, and made them into matching sets for the entire family. In these bright prints, the mu'umu'u came out from undercover, and women began to wear the short style in public. On the Mainland, Hawai'i's statehood in 1959 inspired a college fad for mu'umu'u, while movies such as 1954's *From Here to Eternity* and entertainers from Arthur Godfrey to Tom Selleck have introduced millions to the aloha shirt, or the "Hawaiian shirt," as it is known on the Mainland.

Manufacturers campaigned to launch Aloha Friday in the 1960s, encouraging workers to wear locally made garments and eventually providing a model for the Mainland's Casual Friday. In Honolulu, the aloha shirt became increasingly acceptable as business wear. In the early 1960s, shirtmakers reversed the bright fabrics to produce a shirt of more subtle design, and even made aloha shirts with a button-down collar. Today, a stylish aloha shirt tucked into slacks is the uniform for executives in Hawaii. While many add a blazer for important events or meetings with new clients, formal suits and ties are reserved mostly for lawyers on their way to court.

Businesswomen in Hawai'i are less uniform in their attire, depending on job and location. Honolulu dress tends to be more formal, with some women even wearing suits, pantyhose, and heels. Others, especially on the Neighbor Islands, are a bit more laid back, wearing contemporary Island prints and "dress slippers."

Aloha wear has kept pace with changing fashions over the years, and fabrics today are made with elegant, simple designs, often featuring native plants. An old rayon "silkie," so-called because the fabric feels like silk, is a collector's item and never out of style. "Aloha attire" is requested on invitations to parties, weddings, and even funerals.

The designs have gone beyond clothing, finding a place in fine art and in consumer goods like greeting cards, picture frames, and refrigerator magnets shaped like aloha shirts. There is even a world–record-holding aloha shirt, a size 400XL that hangs in Hilo Hattie's Nimitz Highway store on O'ahu.

Like so much in Hawai'i today, aloha wear draws on many traditions to make up a style of dress that would astonish the noble ladies whose fashion-leader instincts inspired that first holokū nearly 200 years ago.

Footwear

Rubber slippers (also known as "rubbah slippah") are everywhere in Hawai'i, a symbol of the local lifestyle. When did these flip-flops become the official footwear of Hawai'i?

Contemporary Islanders seem to assume slippers have always been here, but old-timers don't remember wearing them in their "small-kid" days. Prewar youngsters went barefoot or, on very special occasions, wore real shoes.

One scholar, Edward Tenner, took a close look at the history of rubber slippers and described their genesis in his book *Our Own Devices: How Technology Remakes Humanity* (2003). Tenner found that Scott Hawai'i, a firm that had made rubber plantation boots for local workers, shifted to rubber sandals when faced with shortages of raw materials during World War II.

Today, these thongs are found around the world and may be upgraded with decorative elements or even high heels. Most folks in Hawai'i, however, stick with the basic rubber slipper and wear a pair until they fall apart, a slipper is lost, or someone accidentally scoops up the wrong pair from the pile by the door after a party.

Humor

One thing I wen' notice 'bout this place
All us guys we tease the other race
It's amazing we can live in the same place

Bob Magoon's song *Mr. San Cho Lee*, adapted and popularized in the 1970s by the Beamer Brothers, pinpointed an aspect of local culture that is sometimes bewildering to newcomers. How the heck can all these people seemingly insult each other and still get along?

Another local entertainer, comedian Frank DeLima, says he thinks this local style of humor actually helped folks live together back in plantation days. Good-natured joking around allowed people with very different backgrounds to defuse tension by laughing at their own and each other's cultural idiosyncrasies.

DeLima is one of several Hawai'i comedians who have raised this comedy to a high art. For 30 years, DeLima has combined accents, costumes, and characters in comic performances that send local audiences into gales of laughter.

Now, DeLima and other local comedians sometimes are accused of racism. DeLima, for one, denies this. "Racism is when a person hates another person because of their race," he says. "I don't hate anybody." This master of ethnic wit cautions others to be sensitive when they are joking around. "Know who you are telling funny jokes to," he advises the students around the state who attend his School Enrichment Program. "You have to know who your audience is. When you don't, you can really hurt somebody."

Fondness and pride are key elements of Hawai'i humor. Our next-door neighbor may have a different accent and eat food that seems a bit strange to us, but we know he is a good guy, and we are proud that these tiny Islands hold so much diversity.

That said, newcomers would do well to remain on the

audience side of the footlights when it comes to local humor. This sort of comedy is a delicate thing, best performed by those who have soaked in Hawai'i's ethnic nuances and know where to draw the line between teasing and insult. Of course, you're welcome to add to the mix by sharing jokes about your own ethnic group!

Likewise, be careful about slang expressions that refer to ethnicity. For example, while some Portuguese people have no problem with calling themselves "Portagee," others consider the word a slur. As with speaking pidgin, it's better for newcomers not to use such terms in an attempt to seem like one of the folks. Be yourself; stick to standard English.

The water cycle

Hawai'i's natural water cycle begins with the trade winds. Moisture-laden winds blowing against steep mountains are deflected upward. As the moisture nears the mountains' peak, it cools and forms clouds, which explains those fluffy clusters hovering around mountain peaks even on the sunniest days.

The clouds' moisture condenses to fall as rain. About 2 billion gallons falls each day on the Island of O'ahu, according to the Honolulu Board of Water Supply. About one-third of that replenishes the aquifer, one-third either evaporates or is used by plants, and one-third runs off. Water can take up to 25 years to percolate through soil and porous volcanic rock to the aquifer below.

On all the Islands, most of the rain falls on the peaks (some of the rainiest spots on the planet) and on the northeastern, windward sides, leaving the leeward sides dry and dependent on piped-in water to thrive.

Hawai'i's native forests are highly effective watersheds. Unfortunately, they have been degraded, beginning with the stripping of sandalwood for trade in the early 1800s. Imported animals such as cattle and pigs have caused far worse damage, ravaging the complex and delicate water-shed and causing erosion. This reduces the amount of water that reaches the aquifer, opens bare ground to opportunistic foreign species, and fills streams with silt and debris that flows into the ocean and smothers reefs.

Foresters understood the importance of watershed as early as the turn of the twentieth century, when the Territorial Legislature created Hawai'i's forest reserve system and began massive investment in forest restoration. Unfortunately, many of the trees planted in forest reserves in the early part of the 1900s were fast-growing, nonnative species, such as eucalyptus, which have produced forests inferior to the complex native ecosystem.

In the 1970s, new state and federal laws were passed to protect sensitive areas and endangered species. Beginning in 1991 with the East Maui Watershed Partnership, public and private entities began cooperative efforts to protect the forest ecosystems that are the Islands' primary sources of water. Similar partnerships now protect hundreds of thousands of acres across the state.

You can help preserve Hawai'i's forests and watershed by volunteering with groups like the Sierra Club or Nature Conservancy to plant trees or uproot invasive species. Clean your boots and gear before a hike so you don't spread unwanted seeds. Don't introduce nonnative animals to Hawai'i or release unwanted pets into the forest. Be careful with fire in the forest (native ecosystems are not adapted to fire and regenerate slowly), and protect streams and drinking water from litter or debris. To learn more or to find volunteer opportunities, visit Mālama Hawaiʻi's Web site at www.malamahawaii.org.

Locals Know: Hawaiʻi is under siege from invasive species. Some of these were deliberately imported, like the mongoose, brought in to catch rats. No one thought about the fact that the mongoose is diurnal, while rats prefer to skulk around at night. Now the mongoose gorges itself on eggs, including those of endangered native birds. Miconia is one of many beautiful plants that arrived as ornamentals and proceeded to take over, threatening to smother native plants. Some things have come in accidentally, like the coqui frog, which apparently hitched a ride on a nursery plant. And no one knows how the Varroa jacobsoni mite appeared, but this little parasite could potentially wipe out the bee population of Hawaiʻi, with catastrophic consequences. Often, it is thoughtless individuals who are responsible for smuggling in plants and animals that have no business here and can cause great harm. Don't be one of those people. And if you can, join in efforts to control the invasive species that are already here.

Caring for the ocean

Do you love the ocean? Perhaps Hawaiʻi's warm blue waters and beautiful beaches are part of what brought you to these Islands. If that is the case, learn to mālama—care for —the ocean, its shores, and its inhabitants.

First, the "don'ts."

Never walk on the reef, which is composed of living creatures and whose health is essential to other living things in the ocean.

Don't litter. Smokers often carelessly discard cigarette butts on the beach, making cigarette filters the No. 1 marine debris item. These can take up to five years to decompose and may be mistaken for food by turtles and other marine life. Plastic also sticks around for years and sometimes mimics food, luring sea creatures to eat debris that will kill them. Plastic may settle on the ocean bottom, smothering coral and other organisms, and eventually will break down into toxins.

Don't bother the wildlife. It can be tempting, when a turtle bobs in the surf, dolphins drift near the shore, or a monk seal suns herself on a beach, to get close for just a little touch. Remember that these animals are wild, and the ocean is their home, not yours; they deserve to be left alone. Touch them, and you are breaking federal law.

Do not feed fish. Giving them bits of bread, frozen peas, or other human food throws the ecosystem out of balance, attracting ugly, aggressive species that drive away the pretty fish you snorkeled out to see. It also dulls their appetite for their natural food, seaweed, allowing the ocean greenery to build up to the detriment of the coral reef.

And now the "do" list.

Clean up after yourself, and even after others, at the beach, and dispose of trash properly. Cut the rings of plastic six-pack holders—sea creatures sometimes get their heads stuck in the rings. Never release helium-filled balloons, which may end up in the ocean looking like food.

Collect only coral fragments that have washed ashore, never live coral from the ocean.

Join the annual International Coastal Cleanup held each September, when volunteers remove litter from shorelines and document what they have found. In Hawai'i, this is called "Get the Drift & Bag It," and it's a good way to have fun outdoors, meet new people, and do a good turn for the environment at the same time.

Locals Know: Don't expect big fancy birds to perch in your back yard. Parrots and other exotic, colorful birds are associated in the popular mind with tropical islands. But Hawai'i's native birds, like its native plants, are smaller and more subtle than those you find in South American jungles. The little birds whose bright feathers were harvested by the ancient Hawaiians to make cloaks, lei, and helmets for the ali'i have been devastated by post-contact predators and disease. Those that survive do so by staying high up in native forests, while the majority of birds in populated areas are imports. A century ago, people thought it was a good idea to bring in pheasants, cardinals, doves, mynahs, and skylarks, among others. We now know better; introducing a new species can tip a delicate ecosystem into harmful imbalance, so don't release exotic birds into the wild. Neuter and control your cats. Hawai'i's native bird population barely survives as it is, without having to fight off feral cats released into the world by irresponsible humans. And get rid of standing water, which breeds mosquitoes, carriers of diseases that devastate native birds.

Saving cultures for the future

Several decades ago, gardeners began to worry about the loss of "heritage" plants. Hybridization had created super crops and a Green Revolution that brought food to many around the world. But some gardeners feared that, in the process of cross-breeding varieties adapted over centuries to their specific locations, humanity was losing important traits in the genetics of vital food plants.

Grandpa's tomatoes might have been smaller, or his corn unlikely to thrive anywhere outside his valley, but those crops were tough, able to survive the insults of their particular environments. Some of their most valuable qualities were lost when scientists cross-bred them with plants from afar.

Just as gardeners began to collect and perpetuate those heritage plant varieties, people of different cultures began to realize that they were losing traits and values their cultures had developed over generations of living in isolated communities. The 1970s saw the "roots" revival in America, with African Americans proclaiming that Black is Beautiful and people of many ethnic groups searching for their family origins.

Hawai'i's native people joined in this search for roots. They launched *Hōkūle'a*, sparking a revival of canoe travel around the Pacific, and with it renewed pride in Polynesian cultures. They brought their language back from the brink of extinction and joined in the music and dance that celebrate Hawai'i's beauty and history.

Increased globalization and economic interdependence are taking people down a similar path all over the world, according to John Naisbitt, the well-known futurist and author of the best-selling *Megatrends* book series. The more interdependent the peoples of the world become, Naisbitt says, the more "tribal" they act, holding onto their cultural identity through dress, stories, language, and a sense of place.

Hawai'i, with its multiple layers of ethnicity, has been on this path for many years. As a newcomer, take advantage of opportunities to sample others' cultures, and at the same time, be proud of your own. Teach your children your family holiday customs, and share them with friends and co-workers. Make that recipe you learned from your German (or Swedish, or Mexican) grandmother for the next neighborhood party. Food, it seems, is the universal language, and a time-honored way to preserve and celebrate cultures.

Globalization may be inevitable, and perhaps even good for the long-term economy of our planet; we'll have to wait and see. But humans cherish their tribal customs and flourish in the village environment. Hawai'i offers an example of a place where traditions survive and enrich a changing world. Like the gardeners who carefully collect the seeds of heritage plants, all of us can preserve the wisdom of people who created cultures that helped them cope with hard times and celebrate good ones.

In the spirit

Spirituality is strong in Hawai'i, whether you find it through experiencing the divine in nature (so deeply felt in this beautiful place that the Hawaiians based their entire religion upon the concept) or through the traditional disciplines of many cultures.

Christian churches abound, as do Buddhist temples. But in Hawai'i, even church has that Island flavor. You may see sacred hula performed as part of a Catholic Mass or enjoy a Tongan choir in an otherwise traditional United Methodist service. Buddhism in Hawai'i has adapted in many ways; congregations often hold Sunday morning services, for example. Jews make up less than one percent of the population, but there are congregations on all the main islands. The Islamic population is very small, mostly centered on a single mosque in Mānoa near the University of Hawai'i.

Those interested in meditation and Eastern spiritual practices will find Hawai'i filled with vibrant communities led by strong teachers offering training in the discipline of your choice. These communities are varied and accessible, ranging from long-established zendos to small meditation sitting groups, from sufi dancing to sweat lodges, from neighborhood yoga classes to an actual Hindu monastery on Kaua'i, and a Tibetan Buddhist stupa (blessed by the Dalai Lama) on Maui. Practitioners of ancient spiritual arts as well as those of more New Age philosophies host retreats in beautiful natural settings around the Islands.

With so many groups devoted to spirituality, it's impossible to list all the connections here. Check the Yellow Pages if you're looking for a mainstream church, or browse for details on the Internet by entering terms such as "Judaism + Hawaii" or "Zen + Hawaii." You will find a wealth of information about the many paths Islanders follow in their search for the divine.

Settling In

Moving to a new place means setting up a whole new routine, finding the services you need, and figuring out all the nuts-and-bolts details of daily life. The early weeks and months can be surprisingly lonely for newcomers who have moved away from family, friends, and people they worked with. Here is a collection of hints and resources to help you get established.

On the Net

Answers to many questions will be found at the following Web sites. If you do not have access to the Internet at home or work, you can connect on the computers at public libraries.

❖ The counties maintain Web sites that can direct you to all sorts of county information, as well as links to various other resources. On the sites you will find sports and recreation opportunities, information on county government, how to reach your county council members, and calendars of events. Parents can link to public and private school Web sites, and on the Honolulu Web site is "Kids World," a collection of links for youngsters that includes lots of help with homework.

❖ The State of Hawai'i Web site is www.state.hi.us. This site includes information about the state's animal quarantine policy, tax forms, how to get a marriage or hunting license, how to register a business, and a Department of Education link with lists of private and public schools and information about home schooling.

❖ Chamber of Commerce Web sites include a number of interesting links, and most offer relocation packets you can purchase online. Enter the island's name and "Chamber of Commerce" in your search engine for the current homepage, and then search for "relocation" within the site.

❖ The U.S. military maintains a comprehensive site for newcomers at www.yourmilitaryinhawaii.com.

❖ Hawai'i Visitors and Convention Bureau offers a collection of year-round events on all Islands at www.calendar.gohawaii.com. Another great site for finding fun stuff: www.hawaiieventsonline.com.

❖ Learn the fascinating history of ancient Polynesian voyagers and their modern counterparts at the Web site of the Pacific Voyaging Society, www.pvs-Hawaii.com.

❖ *Honolulu* magazine regularly "grades" the public schools and runs lists of "the best" doctors, dentists, restaurants, etc. www.honolulumagazine.com.

❖ Hawai'i has about 100 private schools, from pre-kindergarten through college, with tuition ranging from about $3,000 to $12,000 for day students. Many of the schools have waiting lists and require entrance tests and interviews. The Hawai'i Association of Independent Schools Web site includes all their member schools and provides tuition information, contact phone numbers, and Web site addresses for most of them. Consult www.hais.org and the September issue of *Hawaii Business* magazine for details on many private schools.

Who's in charge here?

The voters! But you can't vote if you don't register. Use the form in the phone book or register when you apply for a driver's license.

Hawai'i has two levels of government: state and county. There are no municipal governments, as such, and therefore the entire island of O'ahu, for example, is one unit called the City and County of Honolulu. (This municipality has an unmatched reach—one of its census tracts includes all the Northwest Hawaiian Islands, dozens of tiny islands, shoals, and atolls stretching more than 1,200 miles across the Pacific). Hawai'i's counties were formed in 1905, when the Territorial Legislature passed the law that formed the basis of modern government. It established five counties: Kaua'i, O'ahu, Maui, Hawai'i, and Kalawao. Kalawao was the Hansen's Disease settlement on Moloka'i's Kalaupapa peninsula, then under the jurisdiction of the Territorial Health Department and now a National Historical Park. The four other counties were governed by elected boards of supervisors, later replaced by county councils and mayors.

Perhaps because of the original monarchical government, or the later tradition of centralized plantation operations, the state government established in 1959 retained many traditional county government functions. Hawai'i has the nation's most centralized state government, administering the entire court system, the public health, welfare, correctional, and school systems, as well as all harbors, airports, and major highways.

Honolulu government headquarters is at 530 South King Street in the downtown civic center district, but there are satellite City Hall locations in several places around the island. Check the government pages in the front of the phone book for locations, www.co.honolulu.hi.us.

 Locals Know: Honolulu has a system of Neighborhood Boards that allow each neighborhood to share information and give feedback on community goals and priorities. Members are elected to these boards, which meet monthly.

The County of Maui consists of Maui, Moloka'i, Lāna'i and Kaho'olawe. The nine-story county building is at 200 High Street in Wailuku, www.co.maui.hi.us.

Hawai'i County has two county government head-quarters—one in Hilo, the county seat, at 25 Aupuni Street, and another in Kailua-Kona at 75-5706 Kuakini Street, www.co.hawaii.hi.us.

Kaua'i County's headquarters is at 4444 Rice Street in Līhu'e, www.kauai.gov.

All four counties house various functions in other venues, so check the front pages of your phone book for addresses.

Hawai'i is led by a governor, along with a bicameral legislature composed of a House and Senate. The annual legislative session begins in January. The State Capitol is at 415 South Beretania Street, in the downtown civic center district.

Hawai'i became a state in 1959, thus losing its appointed congressional delegate seat and gaining the right to elect members to Congress—two senators and two repre-sentatives. One represents Hawai'i's First Congressional District—Honolulu and O'ahu's Leeward suburbs—and the other the Second Congressional District—the North Shore and Windward side of O'ahu, and all other islands.

 Locals Know: In Hawai'i, the beach belongs to the people. Private ownership ends at the high wash of the waves, and landowners must allow public access to the shoreline. This right is one of the achievements of former Chief Justice of the Hawai'i Supreme Court William S. Richardson. During his time on the

Hawaii Supreme Court, 1966–1982, Richardson applied Native Hawaiian traditions to law-making in areas such as access to beaches, water rights, and gathering rights. Because of decisions made by his court, water belongs to the public, and Native Hawaiians may enter private land to practice traditional gathering of plants for hula or medicine. Richardson also worked to establish the University of Hawai'i law school, which was named the William S. Richardson School of Law in honor of his work to build an institution that recognizes the importance of diversity and the customs of the Pacific region. Today, the school is small but mighty, widely recognized for its excellence in Asian-Pacific and environmental law.

The state flag

Kamehameha the Great commissioned the Hawaiian flag in 1816, and it has represented Hawai'i ever since. The eight alternating white, red, and blue stripes represent Hawai'i's eight main islands. The British Union Jack represents Hawai'i's historical relationship with Great Britain, which was strong from Kamehameha's days throughout the time of the Hawaiian monarchy.

On the road

Before you try to register your car, you must have 1) proof of no-fault insurance coverage and 2) a current safety check for the vehicle.

And most important: Don't wait to get your Hawai'i driver's license! Trade in your out-of-state license well before it expires. You will need your original Social Security card to obtain a Hawai'i license. Plan ahead! If you do not have the Social Security card, order one immediately so you can get your new license. Some people have run into problems when they either waited too late to renew or did not have a Social Security card and had to wait for one. They then had to take the road test, which can be very tough. You may be able to avoid the road test by doing everything well in advance. Study for the multiple-choice examination by using the official book available in many retail locations or at the public library.

 Locals Know: Drivers and front-seat passengers must wear seat belts at all times or risk a fine. Children under age four must sit in car seats, and those aged four to seven must use a booster seat, unless the child is taller than 4 feet, 9 inches.

Resources for starting a business

Check out the State of Hawai'i Web site for a great collection of information about starting a business—everything from lists of organizations that help small businesses to suggestions for doing a feasibility study to marketing ideas to an overview of business taxes. For example, you must pay General Excise Tax, or GET, on every dollar your business earns (before you deduct expenses!). Get your GET license at the state tax office.

The Hawai'i tax system works a little differently from taxation in other states. Hawai'i is the only state that does not pay for education with property taxes, which makes those taxes seem low compared to the other 49 states. We make up for it in other ways, with income taxes and the GET.

In 2007, the 4 percent GET was increased to 4.5 percent for goods and services on O'ahu. The City and County of Honolulu decided to take advantage of the opportunity provided by a new state law in order to finance future mass transit systems. The other counties chose not to raise the GET rate, but many observers expected the O'ahu rate hike to increase the cost of living around the state. Anyone who buys goods or services from O'ahu vendors will have to pay the extra .5 percent, and the extra tax will be charged on the imported goods that pass through Honolulu.

Pacific Business News, published in Honolulu every week, gives a good overview of business in the state, (808) 955-8100, www.bizjournals.com. Also helpful: the monthly *Hawai'i Business*, (808)537-9500, www.hawaiibusiness.com.

The bad news about business in Hawai'i: The state has the highest costs in the country for doing business, 52 percent higher than the national average, the nonprofit Milken Institute said in 2007. Hawai'i has the country's highest costs for taxes, electricity, and industrial space.

The good news about Hawai'i business? There continue to be opportunities for entrepreneurs who find a niche and work hard to fill it. The annual Made in Hawai'i Festival features everything from soap to sausages to surfboards, and 420 exhibitors at the 2007 event generated more than $1 million dollars during the festival and $10 million or more in residual sales.

 Locals Know: "Don't wait to be successful to give back to the community. Build your career and give back to the community at the same time." That's the key lesson Evan and Kari Leong have learned by talking to dozens of successful business people and community leaders, and they share that lesson and others on their Greater Good Radio show (on ESPN 1420), Greater Good Television (KGMB9), and Web site (www.greatergoodradio.com). This key lesson first came to Evan during a conversation with an influential businessman who said he doesn't undertake any business project unless it helps the community. Now the Leongs make their interviews with top entrepreneurs available through radio, print, Internet, and satellite, so these leaders "can mentor people at a ratio of 1:100,000 instead of 1:1," says Evan. "That in turn will inspire new leaders, and the cycle will continue. We will help develop people's business and entrepreneurial careers and implant a social message and call to action at the same time. We will grow socially conscious business leaders. It is very, very exciting."

Island-style management

Are you the boss? If you just moved Hawai'i to take a management-level position, you may need to be extra sensitive to local ways of doing things. Several high-profile individuals have run into very public trouble in recent years when they let the local welcome go to their heads, while failing to take into account the management style of Hawai'i's long-standing business culture, where an arrogant "make it happen" attitude earns you no friends.

Kama'āina business leaders point out that malihini managers often receive an effusive welcome—hospitality, invitations, even news coverage. If this happens to you, realize it's just Hawai'i's way of greeting any newcomer who, it is hoped, will bring special skills and new ideas. In addition, Islanders are proud of their home, and want to demonstrate immediately to newcomers what a wonderful place this is.

At the same time, that newcomer is being watched to see how he or she reacts to all this adulation, and also how the new manager is able to cope with local ways. Wise ones will do a bit of watching as well, learning by observation how people communicate, what customs they follow, and who the informal leaders are in the group they manage.

New managers who are good listeners, who are willing to learn, and who care about helping the local community will find it easier to fit in. You can't get away from each other on an island, so people often use indirect tactics to deal with disagreements and bend over backward to avoid conflict or anything that would cause others to lose face. Remember, you have entered a pre-existing culture, both business and social, where family ties and long-term friendships mean a lot.

Years ago, I attended a luncheon at which then–Lt. Gov. Jean King was seated with other dignitaries at a long table at one end of the room. As I watched, a waiter worked his way down the table, serving iced tea. When he reached the lieutenant governor, they greeted each other warmly. The waiter and the lieutenant governor hugged, smiled, and talked, clearly renewing old ties. Ever since, this moment has symbolized for me the small-town, all-in-the-'ohana connections that characterize Hawai'i and tend to soften management styles.

One resource to help you understand the gentle, nurturing management that helps preserve Hawai'i's gracious social atmosphere is the book *Managing with Aloha*, by Rosa Say. After years in Hawai'i's hospitality industry, Say put together a management style gained through her own experience and through insights from diverse sources, ranging from traditional Hawaiian values to cutting-edge business books.

Locals Know: Okay, so you expect a kiss when someone greets you with a lei, but what's up with the co-worker who welcomes you with a hug, or the young man who leans over as he shakes your hand to give you a peck on the cheek? This touchy-feely stuff has been the topic of a bit of debate in the past couple of years, especially in business, where sexual harassment is a concern. Some people say the automatic hug-as-greeting is a Hawaiian-style custom expressing aloha. Others, including some who have lived and worked in Hawai'i their whole lives, say hugging and kissing are inappropriate in a business environment and were not common practice in earlier decades. Most agree that a handshake and a smile are the best beginning for a business meeting, but to reduce any awkwardness, watch body language when you meet someone, and be prepared to graciously accept a quick hug. Just knowing that someone may cap an introduction with a hug and maybe a kiss should make it less of a shock when it happens.

Public libraries

"Libraries will get you through times of no money better than money will get you through times of no libraries," according to a poster in my neighborhood library.

Money is usually in short supply for Hawai'i libraries, unfortunately, but they still provide everything from the latest best-seller to free computer and Internet access to a friendly librarian who is happy to help you or your child search for information.

You can borrow a video, listen to a story, send an e-mail, and even renew a passport at some of the state's 51 public libraries. You may borrow books for three weeks and renew them for an additional three weeks if no one else is waiting for them, and you can renew with a phone call to any public library. Check the public libraries' Web site at www.librarieshawaii.org to find out library hours and locations and whether the book you want is in the system (and if that book is on another island, simply request it, and it will be sent to the library of your choice). You can also search the Hawaii Newspaper Index and other databases through this site.

Most of these services are free. All you need is a library card, which you can get at your local library. What can you do to help the libraries? Call your local library to find out about volunteering, and donate books to the Friends of the Library.

And don't forget to return the books you borrow!

Mālama kou kino: health care

The two top health insurance providers in the state are Hawai'i Medical Services Association (HMSA), a Blue Cross/Blue Shield affiliate, and Kaiser Permanente Medical Care Program. HMSA offers several different plans, while Kaiser is a health maintenance organization (HMO). Hawai'i Management Alliance Association (HMAA) and Summerlin Life & Health Insurance Company are the new kids on the block. Hawai'i employers are required to provide health insurance to any worker who puts in 20 hours a week or more. The employer's required contribution to the cost of the coverage must be at least 50 percent but will vary, depending on the business.

While Hawai'i won top rank in a national 2007 study on access to health care because so many residents have insurance, local experts point out that health insurance doesn't do much good if you can't find a doctor. Physicians are especially scarce on the Neighbor Islands, particularly in specialty and trauma care. Dentists are also hard to find. The scarcity is caused by the high cost of living, expensive malpractice premiums, and shrinking reimbursements.

Don't wait until you're sick or have a toothache; connect with a doctor and a dentist as soon as you can, so there'll be an existing relationship when trouble comes. And don't be surprised, if you live on a Neighbor Island, if you have to travel to O'ahu to get care for something as simple as a broken bone; there just aren't enough orthopedists to go around.

Many specialized and advanced services also are available only in Honolulu. If you have an on-going medical problem, ask your doctor about the capabilities of facilities near you. Many Neighbor Island and rural services are handled by the 12-hospital Hawai'i Health Systems Corporation, a semi-autonomous corporation formerly under state control.

Pets in Paradise

Pet owners who move to Hawai'i face some special challenges. First, if you plan to bring your pet with you, you must become familiar with the quarantine laws well in advance of your move. Hawai'i has no rabies, and plans to keep it that way. The quarantine is less draconian than it used to be, but still tough for owners who have not carefully prepared their pet for the move beforehand. For details, check the State's Web site at www.state.hi.us.

Once you're here, be sure to see a vet about medication to protect your dog from heartworm, which is prevalent in Hawai'i and transmitted by mosquitoes. Other services, from microchip identification to spay/neuter surgery, are available from the humane societies on the various islands. These organizations also can use volunteers and donations.

A particular problem is the feral cats sometimes seen around public parks, scrawny and scrounging for food scraps. One way to help with this problem is to sponsor a feral cat colony. Feeding the cats that live in a certain area and making sure that they are neutered gradually decreases the population. You also can rent a trap from the humane society and turn in any cats you catch on your property. If the cat is tame, it may find a home.

One of the biggest problems pet owners face is finding a place to live that will accept their animal. On O'ahu, the Hawaiian Humane Society provides help in the form of its Pets in Housing program. The program offers free materials and forms, including a Pet Addendum to the Rental Agreement, Tips for Tenants, Checklist for Landlords, and Recommendations for Condominium House Rules. The Pet Directory lists buildings on O'ahu that allow pets. The society's Web site, www.hawaiianhumane.org, advertises current rentals that will accept animals. While the directory won't be much help for folks on Neighbor Islands, the other resources for tenants and landlords can be useful no matter where you live.

Kōkua: charitable acts

Many newcomers find that the best way to connect in the Islands is to volunteer. Studies by Hawai'i Community Foundation and others have shown that Hawai'i has a high level of charitable giving and volunteerism, and you'll discover that many of the people you meet are involved in some sort of community activity. Look for others who share your passions, people of like mind, and pitch in.

The United Ways of Hawai'i sponsor a website that

allows you to search for volunteer opportunities that will match your particular talents, interests, and location. Go to www.volunteerhawaii.org to find both ongoing and one-time volunteer opportunities.

One search of the site turned up requests for cleaning, translating, hair styling, accounting, computer tutoring, mentoring, babysitting, making costumes, building homes, tracking dolphins, transporting pets, guiding museum visitors, and staffing fund-raising events, to name just a few. Something for everyone, obviously, so look for the nonprofit organization that needs your talents. What a great way to meet good people!

You can also do good deeds and make friends by attending a rainbow array of events offered by community groups year-round. Many of them benefit nonprofit agencies and other efforts to improve life in the Islands. If you're a golfer, you'll find that there's a benefit tournament somewhere near you almost any weekend of the year, and if you're into dressing up for a fancy dinner, galas abound.

Art lovers will find a wide array of artistic talent on display, and opportunities for music range from jazz to classical to Hawaiian. Regular performances include the slack key series in Kapalua, Maui, and the weekly concerts put on by the Hanalei Family Community Center on Kaua'i. A couple of major film festivals take place each year on O'ahu and Maui, and there are ongoing film events as well. On Lāna'i, the "Stars Under the Stars" film series brings a classic feature film (plus a cartoon!) screened for free under the stars in Dole Park on Lāna'i on the first Wednesday of each month.

Then there are holidays and celebrations unique to Hawai'i or borrowed from other cultures, bringing the world to the Islands. The following Calendar of Events is a mere sampling of ways to have fun. Check local newspapers, the Hawai'i Visitors and Convention Bureau Web site, or the quarterly Kōkua Calendar in *Honolulu* and *Hawai'i Business* magazines for more events, with exact dates, times, and prices.

Locals Know: Many of the fund-raising events put on by Hawai'i charities include auctions and silent auctions featuring bargain-priced gifts, restaurant meals, activity packages, and hotel stays. Buying auction items is a win-win way to benefit a good cause!

Calendar of Events

January

❖ Chinese New Year—Colorful lion dancers and fire-crackers are likely to show up anywhere.

❖ The Narcissus Festival—The Chinese community celebrates the Lunar New Year with a pageant, ball, and other events on O'ahu.

❖ Food Drive Month—Events around the state bring in food and funds for Hawai'i's hungry.

❖ The Starlight Ball benefits the Honolulu Academy of Arts' outreach program for youth at risk.

❖ The Sony Open at the Wai'alae Country Club is the first full-field event of the PGA Tour season, featuring the world's top golfers.

❖ Korean Festival—Experience Korean traditional and contemporary food, dance, music, and cooking demonstrations at Kapi'olani Park in Waikīkī.

❖ Ka Moloka'i Makahiki preserves ancient traditions, especially those specific to Moloka'i, with land and ocean activities, sporting events, lectures, and traditional ceremonies.

❖ Pacific Island Arts Festival—Fine art and handcrafted products, hula, demonstrations of lei making and quilting celebrate the arts of Hawai'i at Kapi'olani Park in Waikīkī.

February

❖ Hawai'i Arts Season starts this month, a time of special emphasis on arts from hula to opera to the Chinese circus. Check the online calendar at www.gohawaii.com/arts for details.

❖ Great Aloha Fun Run, 8.15 miles from Aloha Tower to Aloha Stadium, raises funds for many charities.

❖ Punahou Carnival, at Honolulu's oldest private school, is famous for its games, rides, and lots of food—especially the hot malassadas.

March

❖ Girls' Day—Japanese custom calls for the display on March 3 of special dolls given to girls and passed down through generations.

❖ Art Maui—See the work of Maui's best artists in the annual juried show at the Maui Arts & Cultural Center.

❖ Kona Brewers Festival—Hawai'i and Mainland brewers serve up more than 60 types of micro-brewed beer while chefs offer gourmet cuisine.

❖ Prince Kūhiō Day—Official state holiday honoring Prince Jonah Kalaniana'ole Kūhiō, Hawai'i's delegate to Congress 1902–1922.

❖ Kamehameha School's Song Contest—Hear 2,000 young singers perform Hawaiian songs a cappella in an event that has been going on for more than 80 years. If you can't get a seat in the Blaisdell Arena, enjoy the eight-part harmony on live television.

❖ Great Hawaiian Rubber Duckie Race and Festival—Adopt one of 20,000 rubber duckies that float down the Ala Wai Canal to raise funds for the United Cerebral Palsy Association.

April

❖ East Maui Taro Festival—A weekend celebration centered on the staple Hawaiian plant, with poi-pounding demonstrations, a taro pancake breakfast, crafts, and entertainment in Hāna town.

❖ David Malo Day—A lūʻau and hula honor the Islands' best-known Hawaiian scholar at the school where he studied, Lahainaluna High School.

❖ Spring Gourmet Gala—Kauaʻi Community College Culinary Arts Program benefits from this food and wine-tasting event.

❖ E Mālama I Ke Kai Family Ocean Festival—Bishop Museum hosts a full day of fun for the whole family, with activities and entertainment for a very low price, benefiting Pūnana Leo Hawaiian language immersion programs on Oʻahu.

❖ Merrie Monarch Festival—This week-long cultural event in Hilo culminates in the world championship of hula, with all the best hālau and individual dancers performing in a gorgeous display of skill.

❖ WalkAmerica events this month and next benefit the March of Dimes on each island.

❖ "I Love Kailua Town Party"—Plants, flowers, and produce, activities, entertainment, and "A Taste of Kailua" benefit the Lani-Kailua Outdoor Circle.

May

❖ May Day is Lei Day in Hawai'i—Make or give a lei or at least wear one to any of a number of festivals celebrating Hawai'i's famous garland.

❖ Boys' Day—Many Island families follow the Japanese custom of displaying special boys' dolls and flying carp banners on May 5.

❖ In Celebration of Canoes—Watch islanders from around the Pacific carve canoes, from log to launch, in a Lahaina, Maui, festival that includes arts, a parade, and entertainment.

❖ 50th State Fair—Food, games, booths, and old-fashioned midway rides for four consecutive weekends at the Aloha Stadium on O'ahu.

❖ Filipino Mabuhay Fiesta & Parade—The state's largest Filipino community celebration with headquarters at Kapi'olani Park.

June

❖ Canoe Racing Season—Clubs from around the Islands compete at various sites through September. Watch the sports page for details.

❖ Maui Film Festival Celestial Cinema—Premieres under the stars, with special events and filmmakers' panels at Wailea; includes some films shown on the giant screen in the Castle Theater at the Maui Arts & Cultural Center.

❖ Kamehameha Day—Parades with floats, bands, and Hawaiian-style horseback riders celebrate the king who united the Hawaiian Islands.

❖ Bon dancing—Hawai'i's Buddhist communities remember their ancestors in evening dance ceremonies over the next two months at various Buddhist temples around the Islands. These colorful memorial services are social events with plenty of good food, sold to raise money for the temple.

❖ Hawai'i Salsathon—Dia de San Juan Puerto Rican Cultural and Salsa Festival at Ala Moana Beach Park showcases the Puerto Rican culture and supports the Hispanic Center of Hawai'i.

❖ Kona Marathon, Half Marathon, and 10K/5K Family Fun Run—Choose your running level and follow the beautiful shoreline of the Kona Coast.

July

❖ Annual Paniolo Parade and Makawao Rodeo—Patriotism and the Hawaiian cowboy tradition meet up in the traditional July 4th parade, followed by three days of rodeo events at the Oskie Rice Arena above Makawao, Maui.

❖ Fourth of July celebrations—Fireworks shows change location from year to year; check the newspaper for this year's venue. On Kaua'i, the single largest fund-raiser on the island benefits Kaua'i Hospice with a full afternoon capped with fireworks.

❖ Relay for Life—An overnight event in various locations around the state with participants walking, running, or jogging to support the American Cancer Society's fight against cancer.

❖ Paradise Ride—Bicycle tour of O'ahu, Maui, Kaua'i, and Moloka'i includes full logistical support and entertainment, and benefits a coalition of HIV/AIDS service agencies.

❖ An Evening in Paradise—The Hawai'i Island Chapter of the Hawai'i Hotel Association benefits the Hawai'i Island United Way with wine tasting and food by renowned chefs.

August

❖ Admissions Day—This official state holiday commemorates the day Hawai'i became a state.

❖ American Heart Walk & Health Fair—Employee teams from businesses throughout Hawai'i stroll around Diamond Head or Kapi'olani Park for healthy fun to benefit the American Heart

Association.

- ❖ Honolulu Wine Festival—The largest Italian wine tasting in the nation, plus Italian dishes and live and silent auctions, benefits Hawai'i Lupus Foundation.
- ❖ Plantation Fiesta—The Alexander & Baldwin Museum in Pu'unēnē, Maui, celebrates the good old days of life in the plantation camps.
- ❖ International Bill Fish Tournament—The five-day Kona fishing tournament begins with a party where the captains meet the teams who will fish with them.
- ❖ Hawai'i State Farm Fair—A livestock exhibition, country market, petting zoo, and entertainment at Kapolei Community Park on O'ahu.

September

- ❖ Maui Writers Conference—Hundreds of writers, agents, editors, and publishers gather for four days in Wailea to talk about the written word in a glamorous setting.
- ❖ A Taste of Lahaina—Maui's largest culinary festival, showcasing a variety of restaurants, plus farmers' market, beer garden, cooking demonstrations, kids' games, and music.
- ❖ Honolulu Symphony at La Pietra—Bring a picnic or choose from the food available at this concert under the stars to benefit La Pietra Hawai'i School for Girls.

❖ A Taste of the Hawaiian Range Food and Agricultural Festival—An all-you-can-eat festival featuring
locally produced agricultural products in Waimea on
Hawai'i Island.

❖ Plenty of exercise for runners on Maui this month:
Hāna Relay—a 52-mile relay race on the famous
Hāna Highway; Run to the Sun—it's 36.2 miles from
Kahului to the top of Mount Haleakalā; Maui
Marathon—the big race begins in Kahului and ends
in Ka'anapali.

October

❖ Taste of Kapolei, Ko 'Olina—Enjoy guest chefs,
beverages, and entertainment in this benefit for
programs at Leeward O'ahu schools.

❖ Maui County Fair—A tradition since 1916, the fair
begins on Thursday with a parade in Kahului and
continues through Sunday night with rides, games,
exhibits, entertainment, and food.

❖ Governor's Ball—Honolulu black-tie-optional gala
benefits the March of Dimes Hawai'i Chapter.

❖ Aloha Festivals—Weeks of special Hawaiian events
in various communities with parades, a royal court,
crafts, food, and entertainment.

November

❖ Na Mele O Maui—Schoolchildren compete in a
Hawaiian song contest at Kā'anapali.

❖ Hawai'i International Film Festival—Films from
around the Pacific are shown at various venues.

❖ Hilo Christmas Fair—Now in its third decade, this
craft fair provides grants for community gardens,
scholarships, and support for sustainable local
development.

December

❖ The Queen's Medical Center Auxiliary Annual
Festival of Trees—Local celebrities decorate and

donate miniature trees, which are auctioned off during a sale of handcrafted holiday treasures.

❖ First Light—Maui Film Festival gives audiences an insider's preview of the year's likely Oscar contenders in a week of screenings at the Maui Arts & Cultural Center.

❖ Honolulu Marathon—The annual race takes some 25,000 runners through Waikīkī and past landmarks like Diamond Head and Koko Head. One of the world's largest, this marathon is open to any runner who pays the entry fee.

❖ Mele Kalikimaka—Christmas Island-style includes handcraft sales, the Nutcracker Ballet, Santa in a canoe, and carols accompanied by 'ukulele. Start new traditions of your own; there's nothing like spending Christmas Day on a sunny beach, then calling Mainland friends to report on your tan.

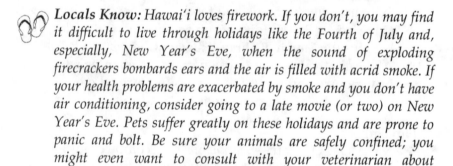

Locals Know: Hawai'i loves firework. If you don't, you may find it difficult to live through holidays like the Fourth of July and, especially, New Year's Eve, when the sound of exploding firecrackers bombards ears and the air is filled with acrid smoke. If your health problems are exacerbated by smoke and you don't have air conditioning, consider going to a late movie (or two) on New Year's Eve. Pets suffer greatly on these holidays and are prone to panic and bolt. Be sure your animals are safely confined; you might even want to consult with your veterinarian about appropriate sedation.

Trouble in Paradise: disaster planning

Hawai'i is not immune to natural disaster and fire. Plan how you'll cope if your area is struck by flood, storm, earthquake, tsunami, or fire. Develop a family evacuation and communication plan. Know which shelter is closest to your home and devise a plan for meeting there if family members become separated. Designate an off-island check-in person everyone can call. Emergency shelters do not accept pets. Leave pets indoors with food and water for most emergencies.

Locals Know: Hawai'i faces a unique variety of natural hazards, from hurricanes to tsunami to lava flows. The University of Hawai'i–Hilo's Center for the Study of Active Volcanoes has created a Web site illustrating the dangers of these hazards and suggesting mitigation strategies to help residents prevent or minimize damage. This terrific site is packed with practical information about how to prepare for and survive these events: www.uhh.hawaii.edu/~csav.

Be prepared

Prepare to get by without power and possibly running water even if you do not have to evacuate to a shelter. Keep at least three days' worth of emergency supplies in your home. Store in sturdy, portable containers:

- ✓ A 3- to 5-day supply of water (one gallon per person per day).
- ✓ A 3- to 5-day supply of nonperishable food. Don't forget the can opener.
- ✓ A change of clothing and sturdy shoes for each person, and a pillow and blanket or sleeping bag for each person.
- ✓ A battery-powered radio, a flashlight, and plenty of extra batteries. Or get one of those crank versions,

where a minute or so of cranking the handle gives you a half-hour of light or radio.

✓ Sanitation supplies and personal items such as toothbrush and soap.

✓ A supply of any medications family members need, extra eyeglasses, and a basic first-aid kit.

✓ Special items for infants, elderly, or disabled family members.

✓ Copies of insurance policies, family records, bank and credit card accounts, and emergency numbers in a waterproof container. Keep an updated inventory and photos of valuable possessions in a safe place.

The warning system

The Civil Defense siren system is tested at 11:45 a.m. the first working day of each month. If you hear sirens at any other time, turn your radio to a local radio station. Listen for emergency information and instructions. Be sure you have enough batteries on hand to operate a portable radio for at least 24 hours in case of power outage. Limit use of the telephone except for emergencies.

Please take "watch" and "warning" announcements seriously. A watch is an official announcement that a hazardous condition may be a serious threat to life and property within a particular time. You should get ready and listen to your radio or television for further instructions.

A warning means that conditions deemed hazardous and life-threatening are about to occur or are occurring. Warning status means take action. The Emergency Alert System will notify you if you should evacuate.

If you must evacuate, keep your family together. Leave a note if some family members are absent, telling them where you have gone. Contact friends and relatives to let them know. Check on elderly or disabled neighbors to make sure they have a safe ride. Turn off electricity, gas, appliances, and water at main circuits and valves. Lock windows and doors.

How to prepare for a hurricane

As many as 13 storms form each year during Hawai'i's hurricane season, between June and November, and storms can also occur at other times of the year. Hurricane Katrina's effect on the Gulf Coast in 2005 and storms that have hit Hawai'i in recent decades prove the incredible power hurricanes have to disrupt life. Hurricane winds, rain, flooding, and storm surge from ocean waves may produce injury and property damage. A hurricane watch means hurricane conditions can be expected within 36 hours. A warning means hurricane conditions can be expected within 24 hours.

When a hurricane is near:

✓ Fill up your car's gas tank, make sure you have cash and credit cards on hand, and check emergency supplies. Keep your cell phone fully charged.
✓ Remove or secure outdoor items and furniture.
✓ Cover or tape windows, skylights, and glass doors. Lock doors and windows.
✓ Store water for drinking, cooking, and sanitation: fill containers, washing machine, sterilized bathtub, and sinks.
✓ Moor boats securely or remove to a safe place.
✓ Unplug appliances except for refrigerators. Turn the refrigerator to the coldest setting and avoid opening the door. Freeze as much ice as possible.

Staying safe from a tsunami

A tsunami is a wave or waves generated by an undersea disturbance such as an earthquake. Waves can grow to great height before smashing into the shoreline, destroying property and anyone in their way. In Hawai'i, more than 200 people have been killed by tsunamis (formerly known as tidal waves) in the past century. Fortunately, Hawai'i is protected by a warning system established in the wake of the devastating April 1946 wave. Although false alarms over the years have lulled Islanders into complacency, the December 2004 tsunami in the Indian Ocean demonstrated the unpredictable power of tsunamis. We're lucky to have a warning system, and should take warnings seriously.

How to survive a tsunami:

- ✓ If you are at the beach when an earthquake occurs, or you see a rapid withdrawal of the sea, head for higher ground immediately.
- ✓ When a tsunami warning has been issued, leave coastal areas immediately, choosing an inland and elevated route.
- ✓ Stay away from the beach and coastal streams. A tsunami may include a series of waves, with later waves even bigger than the first.
- ✓ If you're on a boat, stay at sea until danger has passed.
- ✓ If you have nursed the fantasy of surfing a tsunami, surely the Indian Ocean waves disabused you of that notion. These waves are not for surfing. Do not try.

Flash floods

Flash floods can happen at any time in Hawai'i, and have caused some serious damage. In the event of heavy rain, if you are in a flood-prone area, move to higher ground.

Otherwise, avoid driving if possible, and be careful if you must go out.

If your car stalls in high water, abandon it and move to higher ground. Do not drive in low-lying areas such as those near streambeds.

If floodwaters enter your home, evacuate immediately. If you cannot leave, go to the second floor or roof and wait for help. Take a flashlight, cell phone, radio, and extra clothes.

Wildfire

Hawai'i's dry areas are particularly prone to wildfires. Homeowners should be sure to keep the area around their house clear of dry brush, should learn and teach fire safety practices, store flammable materials away from home, and install smoke detectors.

During a wildfire:

- ✓ Listen to the radio for updates.
- ✓ Remove all combustible items outside the home.
- ✓ Close doors and windows to prevent drafts.
- ✓ Turn off gas valves and pilot lights.
- ✓ Place hoses or sprinklers on the roof.

In the event of wildfires, major highways may be closed. If you're already on the road, tune to a local radio station for updates and instructions.

Earthquakes

Earthquakes come as a surprise. If you've just felt the earth move, you can expect to feel another quake in the near future, but there's no warning before that initial jolt.

It's important, therefore, to think about how you'll react when a quake occurs. In October 2006, residents around Hawai'i experienced a 6.7 quake centered off the Big Island that reminded everyone we live in an active seismic zone, even if we're far from Hawai'i Island's erupting volcano. Hawai'i Island suffered serious structural damage, O'ahu's power-system shutdown created chaos, and one important Maui road was closed for fear of falling rocks.

The Center for the Study of Active Volcanoes' Web site provides detailed instructions for preparing your home and your family to ride out a quake. A few of their suggestions:

- ✓ If you're inside, get under a table, desk, or doorway. Stay away from windows and out of the kitchen. Don't try to rush outside in mid-quake—you might be hit by something falling off the building. If you're outside, keep away from power lines or anything that might fall.
- ✓ Prepare your house (or office) by securing bookshelves to the wall with L-shaped braces; add a "lip" to shelves and child-safe plastic clips to cabinet doors to prevent their opening. Attach TVs and computer monitors to desk or table.
- ✓ Secure your water heater to the house.
- ✓ Reinforce post-and-pier foundations.
- ✓ If you're at the beach, head for high ground.
- ✓ Be sure you have a disaster kit and emergency water supplies, in case there's major damage to your community's infrastructure.

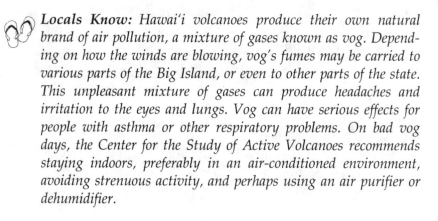

Locals Know: *Hawai'i volcanoes produce their own natural brand of air pollution, a mixture of gases known as vog. Depending on how the winds are blowing, vog's fumes may be carried to various parts of the Big Island, or even to other parts of the state. This unpleasant mixture of gases can produce headaches and irritation to the eyes and lungs. Vog can have serious effects for people with asthma or other respiratory problems. On bad vog days, the Center for the Study of Active Volcanoes recommends staying indoors, preferably in an air-conditioned environment, avoiding strenuous activity, and perhaps using an air purifier or dehumidifier.*

I can't believe how much things cost!

You pay the "Price of Paradise" to live here. It is said that the cost of living in Hawai'i is at least 30 percent higher than on the Mainland, and manager-level salaries are 30 percent lower. Rents are high because the demand for housing has not kept up with the rising population; both land and building supplies cost a lot on an island in the middle of the Pacific. Many people work an extra job (or two) to be able to afford living here.

On the other hand, you may save some on energy bills (no winter heating) and clothing costs (T-shirts, shorts, and rubber slippers will take you a long way here). Entertainment is often free, whether it's a trip to the beach or a few hours at a cultural festival.

Some hints to help you cope:

❖ If you haven't moved here yet, don't automatically ship everything you own—houses here often are small, and furniture is lighter and more oriented to a semi-tropical climate. You might want to wait and pick up what you need once you get here. Moving sales can be full of really nice items (or junk; depends on the sale). Lots of people furnish their places by cruising yard sales on a Saturday morning.

❖ Farmers markets are a great place to save a few bucks on fruits and vegetables, and buying there means you get fresher food and support local growers. Though the main islands each have several markets on different days of the week, here are a few of the best: On Oʻahu, try the Saturday morning market at Kapiʻolani Community College. In Kahului, Maui, the Saturday morning Swap Meet is a great place to pick up all kinds of goodies. The Big Island has many markets, but one of the biggest and best is in Hilo on Wednesday and Saturday. The County of Kauaʻi sponsors Sunshine Markets around the island offering only produce grown on Kauaʻi.

❖ Gasoline? Sorry, we're stuck with some of the highest prices in the country.

❖ Public transportation? Depends on the island. The Bus in Honolulu will take you pretty much anywhere on Oʻahu. Call ahead to 848-5555 to find out what number bus to take and where to transfer. Don't forget to ask about the return trip. On the Neighbor Islands, pickings are slim. Maui County has inaugurated bus service running free loops through the Wailuku-Kahului area and $1 routes to other population centers. Check the county's Web site for routes and schedules, www.co.maui.hi.us. And Maui Economic Opportunity Inc. provides transportation for the elderly, youth, and handicapped; check www.meoinc.org. The free Hele-On Bus will get you around the Big Island, and a shared taxi system takes you door-to-door for as little as $2 in urban Hilo and Kona. Call 961-8744. Kauaʻi Bus offers fixed-route public transportation and door-to-door service for elders, disabled individuals, and some others. Call 241-6410.

❖ Vanpool Hawaiʻi offers one option for commuters. Ride with others for a flat monthly rate plus a share of fuel and parking. The system is available on all islands, but you might have to get a route started. Check www.vanpoolhawaii.com or 596-VANS.

❖ Don't forget you are on an island, and if you want to go to any of the other islands, you'll probably fly. The cost of interisland travel is unpredictable and flights are frequently limited, so plan ahead. You can sometimes find a better deal on interisland tickets if you order through the airlines' Web sites, and some commuter airlines are a bit cheaper.

❖ The ferries from Lahaina, Maui, to Moloka'i and Lāna'i are a bargain, and fun to boot. It's worth a day trip just to see the dolphins frolic on the way and to spend some time at Lāna'i's Hulopo'e Beach or wandering around Kaunakakai. Residents of these islands use the ferries for shopping trips to Maui and sometimes even to commute to work.

❖ The Hawai'i Superferry could change the whole picture of interisland travel, allowing customers to drive their vehicles aboard and off again after an ocean journey to another island. The Superferry was just launching (after a very controversial start) as this edition went to the printer, so by the time you read this, the jury may be in on the Superferry's efficiency and effectiveness. Some people saw it as a boon, like Neighbor Island farmers who want to get their products to O'ahu quickly and cheaply. Some liked the idea of loading the family into the station wagon and heading out for a camping trip or to visit relatives on another island. Others protested the too-rapid approval of a new form of travel that could spread invasive species between the islands, crowd cramped harbors, and contribute to traffic jams on arrival. With so many questions surrounding the ferry's effect (not to mention pending lawsuits), the crystal ball is too cloudy to give you a prediction on this new venture's future.

❖ Also new at press-time: O'ahu's new intra-island ferry from Kalaeloa to downtown Honolulu. A previous ferry on this route failed, but officials began a one-year trial in September 2007 that they hope will work better because improved bus service will transport ferry users to their ultimate destinations in town, Waikīkī, or UH-Mānoa.

- ❖ On any island, you'll find it helpful to plan your shopping trips carefully. Make a list and have a "town day" for shopping and errands; save gas and your nerves by limiting travel time while doing your bit to keep overcrowded roads functioning efficiently.

- ❖ Internet savvy is a big help in the Islands, where you will find less selection in retail stores than you may be used to on the Mainland. Learn to shop online for things you cannot find here. Because the goods will be sent by overnight delivery services, you will probably get things faster than you might by ordering through an on-island retailer who has to wait for a barge to come in. On the other hand, it's nice to shop locally and support the local economy whenever you can.

- ❖ Spend wisely with a little help from *Honolulu* magazine, which frequently runs features on "the best of" everything from auto repair to dentists to restaurants.

Locals Know

Here's a chop-suey collection of suggestions for living on an island.

- ❖ Appreciate the different cultures in Hawai'i. It's a privilege and a joy to live in a place where many different cultures coexist so peacefully.
- ❖ Take off your shoes before you enter someone's house.
- ❖ When you're invited to someone's home for a party or a meal, ask, "What can I bring?" In general, it is good manners to take something when you visit someone. And it is not considered polite to return an empty container—put a little treat, perhaps some fruit from your yard, into those dishes to return to last night's guests.
- ❖ Almost every gathering (including business meetings) includes food, usually far more than is needed, and often guests are sent home with leftovers.
- ❖ Be polite. Be the first to smile. Be humble, not pushy. Do not cut in line. Do not make rude comments about other people's unusual tastes in cuisine.
- ❖ Don't mock the ghost stories you may hear. There is a strong local tradition of spooky stories and reliance on ritual.
- ❖ Do not try to speak pidgin. Period. (Did I mention this before?)
- ❖ Do learn to correctly pronounce Hawaiian words.
- ❖ Learn to pronounce the Hawaiian names of major thoroughfares. With a few exceptions (such as the O'ahu highways known as H-1, H-2, and H-3), no one will know what you mean if you say "Highway 31" instead of "Pi'ilani Highway." Check the street signs while you're at a stoplight and use your waiting time to practice pronouncing the names.
- ❖ Don't call islanders "Hawaiians." Only those of

Native Hawaiian blood, whose ancestors lived here before the 1778 visit of Captain James Cook, are "Hawaiians."

❖ Don't call yourself a "Hawaiian," a "local," or a "kama'āina." "Local" usually means someone who was born and raised here. A kama'āina is a child of the land, usually one who was born in Hawai'i.

❖ Don't refer to the Mainland as "back in the States."

❖ "From water, all things find life." Save water, anywhere you are, no matter where you live, any way you can. Climate changes, or just a run of bad luck, have resulted in very little rain in recent years, and water sources are under great stress.

❖ Don't waste precious water trying to create a rain forest in dry areas of the island. Grow native plants appropriate for your climate.

❖ When it does rain, salt gets soggy, clogging holes in salt shakers. To keep salt flowing, put a few grains of rice into the shaker when you fill it.

❖ When the weather forecast says "kona," close the windows on the south side of the house. Trade winds from the northeast bring most of Hawai'i's rain to the eastern, or windward, side of the Islands. But sometimes the flow reverses: the leeward side gets a soaking, while the northeast side swelters in the still air of "kona weather" without the usual cooling trades.

❖ It's a good idea always to have some emergency supplies on hand—a good stock of canned goods, a few bottles of water, a few weeks' supply of medication, and of course, toilet paper (always the first thing to disappear from shelves when there is a dock-strike scare). It's a long paddle to the nearest wholesaler in case of a hurricane or other disaster.

❖ To keep cockroaches at bay, use the little black plastic discs; date each one and change them every three months on schedule. Or try mixing boric acid with flour for a low-cost roach poison.

❖ Do not kill geckos. Harmless to humans, they eat cockroaches, termites, and other undesirable bugs.

❖ The red dirt in many parts of Hawai'i is famous for staining things, from T-shirts to automobile bodies. Be prepared for things to get dirty. You will need the windows open to let in the trade winds, but along with the breeze comes dust.

❖ Beware of banana blood. The seemingly innocuous clear juice that comes from any part of the banana plant leaves a stubborn stain, so if you're lucky enough to have banana trees, don't mess with them unless you have on your funky garden attire.

❖ Got a tall papaya tree whose fruit is just too high to reach? Go to the hardware store and get an old-fashioned "plumber's helper" and duct tape the rubber plunger to a long pole. Push the plunger against the bottom of the fruit until it breaks off the tree, and lower carefully.

❖ Flowers can be dangerous. A good rule is not to ingest the white sap found in many popular plants. Don't decorate food, or let your kids play, with oleander, plumeria, castor bean, belladonna, or dieffenbachia. And don't eat the mushrooms you find growing in the wild; although some have psychedelic properties, others are just plain killers.

❖ Use common sense around water—as with flowers, nature's beauty can mask danger. At the beach, don't turn your back on the ocean; don't dive into unfamiliar water; stay off the reef; duck or dive beneath breaking waves; and swim across a strong current toward shore rather than into the current. Mountain streams can rise rapidly—if it's cloudy up above you, a flash flood is possible. Don't dive into mountain pools; enter with care, and save your neck and maybe your life.

❖ On a less life-threatening note: Wear sunscreen every day, and don't leave valuables locked in your car at out-of-the-way places.

❖ Obey "no trespassing" signs. Some guidebooks in recent years have encouraged people to climb fences and ignore rules regarding private property, resulting in resentment among local landowners and, sometimes, in people getting themselves into dangerous situations as they wandered into unfamiliar wilderness. Show the same respect and practice the same caution you would anywhere, no matter what that guidebook says.

❖ Remember that we are guests and newcomers in this place. Come here to enjoy the differences and to appreciate the similarities among people. Watch, listen, and learn. There is probably a reason for the way things are done here, and no one appreciates the out-of-state newcomer bent on showing everyone how to get things done. Pitch in and help make Hawai'i a better place to live.

Make New Friends

Here are some strategies newcomers have used to successfully integrate into the Island community.

- ❖ Dan joined a Rotary Club and Toastmasters, and applied for membership at the local country club. He hands out cards with his name and phone number on them, and collects others' names and numbers by having them write on the back of his cards. He then tears off a corner of that card to indicate that it's one to keep, not give away.
- ❖ Sally found joining a canoe club a great way to meet people and learn about the Hawaiian culture, while getting her exercise in a beautiful outdoor setting.
- ❖ Jennifer joined a singing group. She takes yoga classes (from the same teacher, so that she sees the same people in class each week). She attends the potluck gatherings at her condo, and she volunteers at the Humane Society. When Jennifer sent out e-mail invitations for her birthday party, she had a guest list of 60, after only two years on the island!
- ❖ Tony wanted to be active in the community. To prepare himself, he subscribed to the local paper before moving. Once he was here, he spent a full year attending every public meeting he could, sitting quietly, listening and learning, before he felt ready to express an opinion on local issues. "I realized I was an outsider, and assumed I didn't know anything; the people here did. And what's here is better than

what I left behind on the Mainland." And by the way, on the issue of the "old boy network," Tony is reassuring—don't sweat it; it's no different from anywhere else. Do your homework, be willing to listen and to work, and you'll be fine.

❖ Colleen found the best way to get the inside scoop on schools, doctors, and other services for kids was to be an active soccer mom. Getting her kids involved in their favorite sport and hanging out with the parents she met there gave her instant access to many years' worth of wise advice.

❖ David found Hawai'i a "matriarchal society," with many more women in power than he was used to in his native Boston. Some men find it difficult to give up the control they have been used to, both in terms of gender and race and the pace at which things get done. Successful newcomers find it's good to know when to back down and let things go.

❖ Patty and Kent attended a Hawaiian language and culture class through the community college outreach program, and joined a bonsai club to learn how to cultivate the miniature potted plants. These activities put them into immediate contact with two major strands of Island life, the Hawaiian and Japanese cultures. Check with the University of Hawai'i or community college on your island for similar opportunities.

❖ Patty faced medical challenges, and came here knowing the level of care she could receive might not match what she had left behind. "Be clear about why you're coming, and that you may have to get by with fewer medical options," she advised.

❖ Kim joined a Soroptimist Club and spearheaded the planning of a major fund-raising project based on one she had been involved with on the Mainland. This, along with "going next door to borrow sugar," helped her meet a lot of people.

❖ Beth vowed, when she moved to the island, that she

would not turn down any social invitation for at least the first six months. She made many friends and had a lot of fun.

❖ Love Hawaiian music? Sign up for 'ukulele lessons. It's an easy instrument to learn, you'll pick up the correct pronunciation of Hawaiian words from teachers and more experienced students, and you'll make friends while you're making music.

Here is a list of comments collected in a free-for-all discussion among newcomers who have successfully adapted to life in Hawai'i.

❖ Focus on the positive.
❖ Take baked goods to work.
❖ Offer to help if you do something well.
❖ Take your pet for a walk and see how many people stop to say hello.
❖ Try other people's foods. Learn a local recipe to take to a potluck.
❖ Even if it's not a "local" dish, make something for potlucks, don't just take chips and dip. Why not contribute a dish from your own cultural heritage?
❖ Always serve rice. Eat the rice.
❖ Volunteer, volunteer, volunteer.
❖ Buy those sweet bread tickets your co-workers are always selling for their kids' sports team fund-raisers.

Beloved Hawai'i

A strong sense of spirituality pervades the Islands. Perhaps it grows from the original inhabitants' sense of oneness with the land and sea, and the belief that humankind came from the same parents who produced the Islands and everything on them. Hawaiians seek to reach a state known as pono, in which relationships with other people, the land, and God are all in perfect balance. "Pono" is often translated as righteousness, as in the state motto *Ua mau ke ea o ka 'āina i ka pono: The life of the land is preserved in righteousness.*

The Hawaiians' world was devastated by the changes that came after Western contact. When their own chiefs overturned the kapu system that ruled their lives, these spiritually bereft people were open to the new ideas brought by Christian missionaries. Hawaiians adopted and adapted Christianity, retaining many of their ancient customs and beliefs alongside the new ways.

Today, many public gatherings begin with a pule, or prayer. When you hear the phrase, "E pule kākou (let us pray together)," you will know it is time to bow your head for a prayer, often in Hawaiian.

Because of the spiritual connection Hawaiians feel to the 'āina, it is perhaps not surprising that a favorite song, often used to close gatherings, is a hymn in praise of Hawai'i. Written by the Rev. Lorenzo Lyons, a missionary who produced more than 900 hymns in Hawaiian, *Hawai'i Aloha* is probably better known than the official state song,

Hawai'i Pono'ī. Learn the words, and when you hear the song, rise, join hands with your neighbors, and sing along.

Hawai'i Aloha

E Hawai'i, e ku'u one hānau e,

Ku'u home, kulaīwi nei,
'Oli nō au i nā pono lani e.

E Hawai'i, aloha e.

Hui

E hau'oli nā 'ōpio o Hawai'i nei

'Oli e! 'Oli e!
Mai nā aheahe makani e pā
  mai ne
Mau ke aloha, nō Hawai'i

Beloved Hawai'i

O Hawai'i, O sands of
  my birth,
My native home, I
  rejoice in the blessings
  of heaven.
O Hawai'i, aloha.

Chorus

Happy youth of
Hawai'i
Rejoice! Rejoice!
Gentle breezes blow

Love always for
Hawai'i.

You may have seen "Live Aloha" bumper stickers and wondered where these stickers come from and what they really mean.

165

This is the story of the Live Aloha campaign.

In 1993, a group of community leaders on Oʻahu began meeting to talk about how they could improve life in the Islands by reforming government. These were people who had lived in Hawaiʻi all their lives, and they had watched in dismay as the gentle lifestyle they remembered diminished day by day, seemingly lost in the hustle and bustle of modern life. Couldn't government do something to preserve the quality of Island life?

After several meetings, they decided the solution lay less with the government than with individuals, with each person's daily actions.

They decided they would ask the people of Hawaiʻi to agree to undertake certain basic actions in their lives that would encourage sharing, caring, and community building. These would be things that anyone could do, regardless of where they lived or what they did, or how much money or power they might possess.

The group made a list of everyday actions people could take that would express aloha for the world around them. They thought about how to share this list with the public, along with the concept it exemplified, and came up with the idea of a bumper sticker. But what should it say?

Advertising executives volunteered to sit down and brainstorm to find an appropriate bumper sticker phrase. Eventually, their many suggestions were narrowed down to "Live Aloha." The design, by Hilo artist Sig Zane, would include the red ʻōhiʻa lehua blossom, which grows from the barren landscape left by a lava flow, symbolizing the diversity, simple beauty, and enduring strength of Hawaii.

To publicize the Live Aloha campaign, members of the group who worked at television station KHON produced a promotional film, searching their station's archives to come up with material. What they dug up from the past stunned the founders of this modern-day movement.

The producers discovered file footage of an interview with the late Inez MacPhee Ashdown. In 1907, Inez moved from Wyoming to Maui with her father, rancher Angus

MacPhee, who had been hired to manage 'Ulupalakua Ranch. In 1918, MacPhee obtained a lease on the island of Kaho'olawe and began a ranch there. As a young woman, Inez loved being on the island and always hoped that someday she would run the Kaho'olawe Ranch Company.

But when World War II began, Angus MacPhee and his partner, Harry Baldwin, voluntarily turned over the island to the military for bombing practice. Although Kaho'olawe was supposed to be returned to the ranch after the war, the military kept the island and continued to use it for bombing practice. Not until Inez was 94 years old did the federal government return the battered island to the State of Hawai'i for restoration.

Inez had mourned the loss for years. The film clip the Live Aloha film producers discovered was an interview when Inez was in her eighties. She spoke about the bitterness she had felt, and of the spiritual journey she had taken in reconciling herself to the loss of Kaho'olawe.

Inez said she had comforted herself by remembering advice offered by Queen Lili'uokalani. As a child, she had met the queen soon after the MacPhees landed in Hawai'i, when her father was something of a celebrity as a champion rodeo roper newly arrived in the Islands.

Several years later, when Inez was upset by her parents' divorce, the queen took her for a carriage ride one day. "Throw the 'opala [rubbish] from the garden of your heart and let only the golden blossoms of aloha grow there," the queen told the sad little girl back in 1910. "Live aloha."

After watching the promotional film, the Live Aloha group stood silent, many with tear-filled eyes. The motto they had thought a product of contemporary cleverness had in fact been coined decades earlier by a queen whose own losses could have left her bitter. As the last monarch of Hawai'i, Lili'uokalani had seen her kingdom overthrown in 1893. After her country was annexed by the United States in 1898, Queen Lili'uokalani might have spent the rest of her life in anger and regret.

Instead, Lili'uokalani chose to live and teach aloha.

Now, somehow, the queen's heartfelt advice to an unhappy child had resurfaced to help a modern community connect to the ancient values that continue to make Hawai'i unique.

More than 600,000 Live Aloha bumper stickers have been distributed, many to schoolchildren. Each comes with a card describing the kinds of actions the Live Aloha founders identified as exemplifying the attitudes and way of life that make Hawai'i a special place.

From the Live Aloha card, here are some suggestions:

- Respect your elders and children.
- Leave places better than you find them.
- Hold the door. Hold the elevator.
- Plant something.
- Drive with courtesy. Let others in.
- Attend an event of another culture.
- Return your shopping cart.
- Get out and enjoy nature.
- Pick up litter.
- Share with your neighbors.
- Create smiles.
- Make a list of your own.

If you aspire to "live aloha" in your new home, remember these suggestions offered by a group of people who have loved Hawai'i their whole lives, and whose modern-day efforts somehow tapped into the stream of wisdom flowing from the spirit of Hawai'i's last queen.

To obtain your own bumper sticker, send a No. 10 stamped, self-addressed envelope to Live Aloha, 165 Waokanaka Place, Honolulu HI 96817. Although there is no charge for the bumper sticker, if you would like to support this campaign and the printing of more bumper stickers, include a check made out to the Hawai'i Community Foundation, with "Live Aloha Fund" in the memo line.

"We Live on an Island"

The following is an excerpt from a "chicken-skin" speech given by Audrey Rocha Reed to the Maui Chamber of Commerce when she won the T. S. Shinn Award for community service in June 2003. Hearing about Audrey's work with the community through her job, running the J. Walter Cameron Center (headquarters for a number of Maui nonprofits), and her other activities will give you a feel for how people work together in the Islands. And you'll get a sense of life in the Islands in the plantation community, where life was simpler and people knew and cared for one another. I can find no better description for how to "Live Aloha."

We live on an island. Islands are limited in resources—and unlimited in possibilities to make things work. Because we're limited, we tend to be thrifty—to make do with what we have; to manage well. Because resources are limited, we know one another —we know who can do what—and when we pull together, we can make things happen here that could never happen in larger places.

The Special Fair is an example of this. Since 1990, we've managed each year to take people with disabilities to the Maui County Fair for one special day. The first year, we had about 400 guests and an equal number of volunteers. The event has grown each year. Last year, there were over 1,000 special guests and 1,100 volunteers. Maui Economic Opportunity and student transportation commandeer every vehicle on the island capable of transporting wheelchairs. We invite [long-term-care] residents of Kula Hospital and both Hale Makua facilities. We have special guests from Moloka'i topside and Lāna'i. We include those on dialysis, on crutches, and for the last three years, we've been able to include 18 former patients from Kalaupapa.

We persuade top entertainers to donate their talent at the Special Fair. Businesses, nonprofits, and the Maui County Fair contribute money to purchase food and souvenirs. Hale Mahaolu's staff holds a fund-raiser to come up with a donation of $1,000 each year—and then, Hale Mahaolu cooks the chili and much of the rice we need. Maui Toyota pays for all the chili ingredients. Maui Soda & Ice donates ice cream; Wailuku Hongwanji cooks and donates chow fun. Sons and Daughters of the 442nd barbecue 400-plus pounds of chicken. The Boy Scouts donate pronto pups. Last year, we fed over 2,000 people at the Special Fair.

E. K. Fernandez rides are provided free to the disabled fairgoers. Other volunteers come from St. Anthony High School, the Volunteer Center of Maui County, the Lions and Kiwanis clubs, and even the inmates of Maui Community Correctional Center. Lawmakers and lawbreakers both team up to put on the event. We succeed where no other place does because Maui is special. We live on an island where we know and appreciate one another. We understand how lucky we are.

I was born almost sixty-two years ago at the old Pā'ia hospital. I grew up in a plantation camp—Hāmākuapoko. Most of us called it simply H'poko.

A plantation camp was very much like an island—limited in resources, size, population. Everybody knew everybody else—our strengths and weaknesses, in sports, in school, in cooking, in raising animals, tending gardens, sewing, and playing marbles. It took me many years to really comprehend how unique our lifestyle was.

To wake up in the morning and find a bunch of bananas, or avocados, or onions on the back porch—no note; donor unknown. Or to go to the little field in our camp to celebrate Rizal Day with our Filipino neighbors and to eat pork and peas, and listen to their music and watch them dance.

To know, without ever being told, that you take your slippers off before you go into someone's home. To wait during the evenings before Christmas for the Puerto Ricans to come singing their aguinaldos—and watching my father pour little glasses of wine to help them sing even better. And to wait for sushi at New Year's from our Japanese friends.

ISLAND LIFE 101

To wake up early on a Tuesday morning in spring and smell malassadas frying—and to get dressed quickly so I could deliver my mother's malassadas hot to our neighbors and friends all over the camp. And often, I'd run into my cousins and nieces on the same errands for their mothers.

When our softball team or basketball team played against teams from other camps, we went to the games and cheered our players on. We went to every wedding regardless of who was getting married, and usually Hawaiian food was served; we celebrated birthdays, and comforted each other at funerals. We helped each other out.

Plantation camp life taught me this: to be loyal first to family and not bring them shame, to be loyal to friends and to respect their cultures, to share any bounty I might have with others, to be honest, to work hard, and to step forward when asked to help. These are the lessons everybody in a plantation camp learned. . . .

Glossary

Note: Hawaiian words often have more than one meaning. The simple definitions below refer to the way the words are used in this book; expanded definitions and additional meanings may be found in the *Hawaiian Dictionary* (Pukui and Elbert).

ahupua'a—A land division in ancient times, often running from the mountains to the sea.

'āina—Land, earth; "that which feeds us."

ali'i—Chief, chiefess, noble, royal.

aloha—Love, affection, compassion, greetings, farewell.

'aumakua—Family or personal god.

camp—In Hawai'i, this common English word refers to plantation villages where housing and many other necessities were provided by the company.

E pule kākou—"Let us pray together."

hala—The pandanus tree, whose leaves (lau) are used to make lau hala mats or hats.

hala kahiki—Pineapple, or foreign hala, so called because the pineapple resembles the fruit of the hala tree. "Kahiki," the Hawaiian pronunciation of Tahiti, refers to any foreign country.

hānai—Foster or adopted child.

haole—Foreigner, usually a white person. In ancient usage, anything of foreign origin.

heiau—Pre-Christian place of worship.

ho'okipa—To entertain; welcome; offer hospitality.

kahakō—The macron, as seen above the final "o" in this word; used to indicate that a syllable is stressed.

kahiko—Old, ancient, old person; the old style of hula.

kahuna—Priest, minister, expert in any profession.

kalo—Taro, the staple plant of Hawai'i. Its root is used for poi, and its heart-shaped leaves (lū'au) are cooked as greens.

kama'āina—Native born, host, native plant, familiar. Literally, "land child."

kanaka—Human being, man, individual, mankind.

Kanaloa—One of the four great Hawaiian gods. The others are Kāne, Lono, and Kū.

kane—Man, male, husband.

kapa—Tapa, a papery cloth made from the bark of the wauke or mamaki tree.

ka po'e—People, persons, group. "Ka po'e kahiko" means "the people of old."

kapu—Taboo, forbidden; also sacred, holy, consecrated.

kauwā—Untouchable, outcast, slave, servant.

kōkua—Help, assist, comfort.

kuleana—Small piece of property within an ahupua'a; r esponsibility, right, jurisdiction.

Kumulipo—Hawaiian creation chant.

kūpono—Upright, proper, fair.

kupuna—Grandparent, ancestor, relative of the grandparents' generation.

lo'i—Irrigated terrace where kalo (or rice) is grown.

Lō'ihi—Length, height, long; name given to a new island forming under the sea east of Hawai'i.

lōkāhi—Unity, agreement, accord.

māhele—Portion, division; the Great Māhele of 1848 divided land into portions for personal ownership.

maka'āinana—Commoner, populace, citizen; the "eyes of the land."

mālama—To take care of, care for, preserve.

mālama kou kino—Take care of your body.

malihini—Stranger, newcomer, guest.

mana—Supernatural or divine power.

maoli—Native, indigenous.

mele—Song, chant, poem.

Neighbor Islands—The populated islands except for O'ahu. Neighbor Islanders usually prefer this term over "Outer Islands."

'ohana—Family, relative, related.

'okina—Cutting off, separating; the glottal stop, symbolized by '. May begin a word, as it does *'okina*, or be inserted between two vowels.

oli—Chant that was not danced to.

'olu'olu—Polite, kind, courteous,pleasant.

'ono—Delicious, tasty; to be 'ono for a food is to crave it.

paniolo—Cowboy. Probably from "español."

Pele—The volcano goddess.

pidgin—A mixed language incorporating the vocabulary of one or more languages. Hawai'i vernacular is actually a creole descended from the pidgin used by early settlers.

pono—Goodness, uprightness, righteous, proper.

wahine—Woman, female, wife.

wai—Fresh water, liquid.

waiwai—Goods, property, wealth, rich.

Recommended Reading

Adams, Wanda A. *The Island Plate: 150 Years of Recipes and Food Lore from the Honolulu Advertiser.* 2006. Honolulu: Island Heritage Publishing.

Ainsworth, Gail, and Bren Bailey. *Maui Remembers: A Local History.* 1995. Honolulu: Mutual Publishing.

Arthur, Linda B. *Aloha Attire.* 2000. Atglen, Pa.: Schiffer Publishing.

Ashman, Mike. *Kauai: As It Was in the 1940s and '50s.* 2004. Līhu'e: Kaua'i Historical Society.

Beckwith, Martha. *Hawaiian Mythology.* 1970. Honolulu: University of Hawai'i Press.

Bird, Isabella L. *Six Months in the Sandwich Islands.* 1998. Honolulu: Mutual Publishing.

Blackford, Mansel. *Fragile Paradise: The Impact of Tourism on Maui, 1959–2000.* 2001. Lawrence: University Press of Kansas.

Cahill, Emmett. *The Life and Times of John Young: Confidant and Advisor to Kamehameha the Great.* 1999. Honolulu: Island Heritage Publishing.

Chiddix, Jim, and MacKinnon Simpson. *Next Stop Honolulu! Oahu Railway & Land Company, 1889–1971.* 2004. Honolulu: Sugar Cane Press.

Ching, Carrie. *Things Hawai'i.* 2004. Honolulu: Mutual Publishing.

Clarke, Joan. *Family Traditions in Hawai'i.* 1994. Honolulu: Namkoong Publishing.

Cook, Chris. *Kaua'i, the Garden Island: A Pictorial History.* 1999. Virginia Beach, Virginia: The Donning Company.

Cooper, George, and Gavan Daws. *Land and Power in Hawai'i.* 1990. Honolulu: University of Hawai'i Press.

Daws, Gavan. *Shoal of Time: A History of the Hawaiian Islands.* 1968. Honolulu: University of Hawai'i Press.

Elbert, Samuel H., and Noelani Mahoe. *Nā Mele o Hawai'i Nei.* 1970. Honolulu: University Press of Hawai'i.

Engledow, Jill, and Mary Cameron Sanford. *The Maui News: One Hundred Years as Maui's Newspaper.* 2000. Wailuku, Hawai'i: Maui Publishing Co.

Fuchs, Lawrence H. *Hawaii Pono: An Ethnic and Political History.* 1961. Honolulu: Bess Press.

Harden, MJ. *Voices of Wisdom.* 1999. Kula, Hawai'i: Aka Press.

Joesting, Edward. *Kaua'i: The Separate Kingdom.* 1987. Honolulu: University of Hawai'i Press.

Kame'eleihiwa, Lilikalā. *Native Land and Foreign Desires.* 1992. Honolulu: Bishop Museum Press.

Kanahele, George S., ed. *Hawaiian Music and Musicians.* 1979. Honolulu: University Press of Hawai'i.

Kāne, Herb Kawainui. *Ancient Hawai'i.* 1997. Honolulu: The Kawainui Press.

Loomis, Albertine. *Grapes of Canaan: Hawaii 1820, The True Story of Hawaii's Missionaries.* 1998. Woodbridge, Conn.: Ox Bow Press.

McDermott, John F., Jr., Wen-Shing Tseng, and Thomas W. Maretzki, eds. *People and Cultures of Hawaii: A Psychocultural Profile.* 1980. Honolulu: University of Hawai'i Press.

Oaks, Robert F. *A History of the Big Island.* 2003. Charleston, S.C.: Arcadia Publishing.

Polancy, Toni. *So You Want to Live in Hawai'i.* 1998. Kīhei, Hawai'i: Barefoot Publishing.

Pukui, Mary Kawena, and Samuel H. Elbert. *Hawaiian Dictionary.* 1971. Honolulu: University Press of Hawai'i.

Pukui, Mary Kawena, Samuel H. Elbert, and Esther T. Mookini. *Place Names of Hawai'i.* 1974. Honolulu: University Press of Hawai'i.

Silverman, Jane L. *Kaahumanu: Molder of Change*. 1987. Honolulu: Friends of the Judiciary History Center of Hawai'i.

Simonson, Douglas, et al. *Pidgin to da Max*. 1981. Honolulu: Bess Press.

Ten Bruggencate, Jan T. *Hawai'i's Pineapple Century: A History of the Crowned Fruit in the Hawaiian Islands*. 2004. Honolulu: Mutual Publishing.

Tenner, Edward. *Our Own Devices: How Technology Remakes Humanity*. 2004. New York: Vintage Books.

Trask, Haunani-Kay. *From a Native Daughter: Colonialism and Sovereignty in Hawai'i*. 1999. Honolulu: University of Hawai'i Press.

Wilcox, Carol. *Sugar Water: Hawai'i's Plantation Ditches*. 1996. Honolulu: University of Hawai'i Press.

Index

About the Author

Jill Engledow began her Island life at age thirteen, when she moved with her family from Texas to Hilo. Jill fell in love with Hawai'i—its land, people, music, and culture. After she arrived on Maui, in 1968, this love affair with the Islands blossomed into a committed long-term relationship.

Jill's writing has chronicled Maui life for thirty years, most notably during her seventeen years at *The Maui News*. An award-winning journalist, she is also author or co-author of several books about the history of Maui.

Island Life 101: A Newcomer's Guide to Hawai'i began as a photo-copied handbook for the *Island Life 101 Seminars*, which Jill developed as a way to help newcomers to the Islands understand and connect with the history, culture, and community life of their new Island home. She has presented the *Island Life 101 Seminar* to groups on Maui and O'ahu.

To Order

Island Life 101:
A Newcomer's Guide to Hawai`i

Send $17.95 plus $4.60 Priority Mail shipping to:

Maui Island Press
P.O. Box 176
Wailuku, HI 96793-0176

Telephone (808) 242-5459

Please send me_____copies of

Island Life 101: A Newcomer's Guide to Hawai`i

Name_____

Address_____

City_____State____Zip_____

Telephone_____

E-mail address_____

Number of copies:_____ × $22.55 ($17.95 + $4.60) =

_____